UNITY LIBRARY & ARCHIVES
The testament of truth
BF 1999 .T68

THE TESTAMENT OF TRUTH

By the same author
The Wisdom of the Spirit
The Science of Wisdom (3 vols)
Solution to the Riddle
The Philosophy of the Spirit
The Fire of Knowing

THE TESTAMENT OF TRUTH

By Clarice Toyne

Foreword by W. R. Matthews
Dean of St Paul's Cathedral

London · George Allen & Unwin Ltd
RUSKIN HOUSE MUSEUM STREET

First published in 1970

This book is copyright under the Berne Convention. All rights reserved. Apart from any fair dealing for the purpose of private study, research, criticism or review, as permitted under the Copyright Act, 1956, no part of this publication may be reproduced, stored in a retrieval system, or transmitted, in any form or by any means, electronic, electrical, chemical, mechanical, optical, photocopying, recording or otherwise, without the prior permission of the copyright owner. Enquiries should be addressed to the Publishers.

© George Allen & Unwin Ltd, 1970
ISBN 0 04 291005 6

Printed in Great Britain
in 11 point Baskerville type
by Clarke, Doble & Brendon Ltd
Plymouth

*To those who shared with me this high adventure—
with love*

Contents

Foreword by W. R. Matthews, Dean of St Paul's Cathedral	*page*	11
Preface		13
1. Childhood and Youth		15
2. High Adventuring		30
3. Awakening		48
4. New Paths		53
5. Life Saving		59
6. Profit and Loss		63
7. The Celestial Visitor		66
8. Further Interviews		86
9. Mountain Slopes		100
10. Darkness		108
11. The Rays		111
12. Seeing		117
13. Progress and Publication		123
14. Understanding and Frustration		137
15. Light and Darkness		143
16. Chronicles of Fire		151
17. Dreams and Symbols		162
18. Renewal or Reincarnation		169
19. The Path of a Soul		180
20. Flashbacks		183
21. Opportunity and Plans		186
22. Fulfilment		193
23. The Open Church		197
Epilogue		203

The human heart can go the lengths of God.
Dark and cold we may be, but this
Is no winter now. The frozen misery
Of centuries breaks, cracks, begins to move;
The thunder is the thunder of the floes,
The thaw, the flood, the upstart Spring.
Thank God our time is now when wrong
Comes up to face us everywhere,
Never to leave us till we take
The longest stride of soul men ever took.
Affairs are now soul size.
The enterprise is –
Exploration into God.

CHRISTOPHER FRY

Foreword

*The Deanery, St Paul's
London E.C.4.*

17th January, 1958

Dear Mrs Toyne,
 I have read your MS. and found it interesting.
 I think that if it is to be given to the world by publication in book form, the question which will be in every reader's mind is, How does the author know all this? And of course the answer is that it came to you by what seemed to be a kind of revelation or series of visions. It seems to me, therefore, that it is essential that this should be clearly stated and that you should give a clear account of how this came to you—I mean in some detail.
 Do you think you could do this?

Yours sincerely,
W. R. Matthews
(Dean of St Paul's Cathedral)

Preface

Some years ago, Dr Matthews, Dean of St Paul's, having read the first book of my Trilogy, *The Science of Wisdom*, and after a talk that we had together, wrote asking me to write, as he said, 'in some detail', of the experiences which led to my formulating what might be called the religious philosophy of the 'New Understanding'.

I hesitated. Such a work seemed to me presumptuous and overloaded with the ego.

However, of late, others have made the same request, so that I felt bound to tackle the task. Remembering that where such things happen to one they happen to many, I have given the kind of spiritual experiences which I hope will help those who are seekers after further understanding, who are struggling up the same glassy mountain, the ascent of the consciousness into the inner dimensions.

In our time men and women have lost a sense of purpose. Some have come to think that human beings are the result of a chance coming together of chemicals, of no more significance than a meteorite, and as easily quenched. In this dark concept lies the inevitable sinking of man's noble endeavour, the halting of his effortful drive forwards. That which came to me in the ways which I shall describe shows beyond doubt that man stands at the peak of natural development, and that the curling billows of his evolution bear him onwards upon a tide of majestic expansion, both in power of thought and spiritual adventure. He is at the crest of nature's wave, and this forward-thrusting is inherent in the pattern of things which is in its essence divine. We are eternal in our individual being and in our progress – if we would have it so.

In explaining how this understanding came to me there stands exemplified the truth of a saying which was dropped into my mind one day:

'You are cherished beyond your knowing.'

And this is true of all of us.

It is because I have been so amply and continuously helped to prove the truth of this saying that I wrote this book, to demonstrate that which this new understanding offers – courage, comfort and a splendid hope.

Chapter One

CHILDHOOD AND YOUTH

1

It has always been the texture of life which fascinates me most. From earliest childhood I remember noticing a strange phenomenon. If one were to sit still, relaxed and absorbent of the atmosphere, the pattern of reality around one would take a sideways quirk, as it were, and the familiar room, the furniture, the hangings, the pictures in their frames, would shimmer suddenly and take on a new appearance.

What I saw on those occasions would differ in quality and texture, in substance, form and the slant of light, in the same relationship as the French Impressionist pictures differ from the firm outline of a Dutch Interior. And it was thus that I came to know two worlds. One side of my nature relished and journeyed in the world of clear light and sharp detail as of a Dutch Interior, the world of outside things, while the other sought for and often experienced the patterned sunlight and shadows and the blurred outlines of a Manet or a Corot, or the electric burning quality of a Van Gogh. Both were real. Both had their especial enchantment. Yet I grew to realize that both were merely outer husks, the matrix upon the diamond which lay deeper within.

Absolute stillness and quiet lit the way inwards, towards those inner dimensions.

When I was about seven years old, life provided me with the most rewarding interlude in the form of a long idle convalescence, during which there was plenty of time for these excursions of the mind. Although I was a stalwart child and neither before nor afterwards was wont to have a day's illness which could keep me in bed, and neither my brother nor I took any of the usual childish infections, yet suddenly I was smitten with swollen glands in the neck. My temperature rose and I was banished to bed. Absolute rest was prescribed. And because the recalcitrant fever refused to abate, there I remained for a period of many weeks. Indeed, some months of mellifluous spring and summer sunshine found me still in bed, or made to rest upon a *chaise-longue* in the garden with no movement. As far as I remember I felt neither illness nor pain, but I was able to laze the livelong day, suspended as it were between the world of action and the world of dreams.

My mother cherished me tenderly, and kept me amply provided with books and comic papers, but when these were laid aside this period of enforced inaction was in fact of the utmost benefit to me. I discovered that there was a scintillating world of enchantment and of kaleidoscopic ideas – aside from the world of 'doing' – to be experienced through half closed eyes or through the subtler antennae within. The way of withdrawal into a turret room of the mind opened a skylight into a realm of reality undreamed of from the ground floor level.

The termination of that illness was spectacular, and no doubt played a part in shaping my life.

The swollen glands persisted and my parents became alarmed.

One day two doctors came. A second opinion had been thought desirable. They conferred in another room and then went away. My mother's eyes looked dark with anxiety, though I had no idea what was toward.

A long time later she explained.

The doctors had declared that an operation was necessary. The offending glands must be cut away. My mother had begged that a stay of execution be granted. Let them wait one more day before they fixed their decision . . . just twenty-four hours longer. The doctors reluctantly agreed and went away.

My mother went to her room to pray. She told me that she had prayed earnestly all night long.

And lo, in the morning the swelling had disappeared. The neck was smooth and clear and when the doctors returned they were amazed. The temperature was normal, and soon I was up and about.

The little object lesson no doubt was partly the basis of my subsequent absolute faith in prayer.

2

I was born in August 1906.

My parents at that time had a worthy house in Hampstead. There we remained until 1913 when a kindly Providence removed us from the prospect of wartime London and air raids, out into the healthy countryside of Surrey.

Though we left it when I was five years old, I well remember that Hampstead house, chiefly for its lights and shades, its textures and atmospheres. To children the hard outline of things, the 'Dutch Interior' aspect of life scarcely matters. What is of paramount importance is the smell of things and the pattern their shadows take. Indeed, on reflection, it seems to me that my awareness of life at that time falls clearly into the chequer-board pattern of 'light things' and 'dark things'.

Characteristic of Edwardian London, that house where I lived for the first five years of my life was four-storied and – to me – gloomy. My brother and I occupied the top floor. Here was night nursery, day nursery, our nurse's and later our governess' room, the 'gas room' and the 'glory hole'.

These memories are loaded for me still with vague disquiet. In the night nursery it was always night. Did the dawn never break into that dark room? If it did I don't remember it. The word 'night' and the gloom of being left alone in that back room still hangs a panoply of Stygian darkness over my recollections. My brother, being three years older than I, presumably went to bed long after sleep had rescued me from that nightly vigil – though a night-light usually burned an oasis of gold into the pall of black velvet around my bed.

The 'gas room' effused a grey shadow over our landing. Presumably it was merely a little pantry where tea might be brewed and the nursery crockery washed up, but it had an appearance of grey lead, that being the period before bright porcelain sinks cheered such necessary tasks.

The 'glory hole' was a horror.

Its ink-black cavity was never lit by electric light nor candle, and if its door inadvertently was left open, one stared into impenetrable darkness. Presumably it contained the boxes, trunks and usual clutter of a lumber room, and if I had once been shown its homely contents I should have been comforted. As it was, however, the knowledge of that lightless cavity and the mystery of its name, dominated our landing, even were the door kept closed. No doubt these brooding shadows stimulated my insatiable and secret longing for 'all things bright and beautiful'.

Our day nursery faced the garden. I suppose the sun shone sometimes but, strange to say, I only remember rain. I used to sit curled up on the window-seat of the nursery looking with faint dismay at the small circles of water plopping upon the flat roof of an outhouse below us, which my mother, to comfort me, said were 'only sailor boys dancing in the rain'.

Perhaps the last months of our stay in the house were unusually wet, for somehow the impression which remains with me is dim and monochrome. One bright picture, however, remains sharp on the screen of my mind. The nursery tea table each day would be set with patterned china which caused the spirits to lift and the heart to glow. The cups and plates were decorated with gay designs of formalized flowers in vermilion and yellow, and these, upon the white cloth, with the accompaniment of dancing firelight behind the brass-edged fireguard, set the mind tingling.

In those days children were not allowed the run of the house as in later times. We either were taken for walks, or we played upstairs. On certain startling occasions, when my mother had a tea party, we were polished up and taken downstairs. The drawing-room door would be pushed open and we were thrust over the threshold into a mist of chatter and faces and poised teacups. My mother would draw us to her, dressed in a long flounced cream lace gown, with a rose tucked in her corsage, and her vital dark hair piled high upon her fine head. Her dark, full eyes were bright and tender, and her lips curved with gentle laughter. My mother to me was 'bright and beautiful'.

At these tea parties we were forced by courtesy to entertain my mother's guests. My brother Rex, resplendent in a white sailor suit, with long trousers, and a whistle on a lanyard proudly tucked into his tunic, recited 'The Boy stood on the burning deck'. Then I, in my best party dress of white muslin with a pink sash, solid and four years old, repeated a nursery rhyme.

On Sunday evenings we would again be fetched downstairs, this time to sing hymns around the piano. This was a highlight in the week. My mother had a warm singing voice and she played the piano in masterly style, while my father had a light baritone and he sang with gaiety and verve. Grouped around my mother, while my eyes wandered over the fretted woodwork of the piano front, interlaced as it was with a gold plush lining, we sang the old sweet children's hymns.

> 'I love to hear the story
> Which angels' voices tell. . . .'

And all sense of gloom which sometimes burdened me upstairs would fade away, and I would stand for a while in a pool of light – or so it seemed to me – which nothing could assail.

Yet sometimes troublous storms blew up.

We had at that time a sinister old cook. Perhaps even in those days domestic staff was not always easy to come by, but this cook became a menace to us children. She used to tease my brother Rex continually, though I never remember her baiting me. She would loom from the lower regions where the kitchens were, and call after us as we went primly through the hall with our nurse, to take the air on Hampstead Heath, hoops in hand – mine, of course, a mere wooden one, while Rex's was of masculine iron. She jeered that in his large straw sailor hat Rex 'looked like a tom tit on a round of beef'. I never understood the reference, nor could see that Rex looked in the least bit like the bird or the joint in question. We would scuttle out into the street glad to get away from the old harridan. On one occasion she surpassed even her teasing ways. In our nursery there stood a chest of no particular dimensions, and into this she packed my screaming brother – for some small misdemeanour – and seated herself firmly upon the closed lid.

I was too frozen with terror to stir in his defence, and wondered why our governess made no attempt to dislodge her. Cook sat firm, undaunted by Rex's muffled howls.

However, somehow or other my parents must have heard of this misadventure, for after a while we saw that cook no more. We had a series of housemaids or nursemaids whom I found more congenial company. My father complained that 'these girls were always going off and getting married', but while they were with us they gave us some of their cheerful company, in their laughing ways, their white aprons and frilly caps with streamers flying out behind, picking raspberries in the garden and having secret feasts among the laurels.

'Aldy' (called Aldworth by my parents) took us for walks each afternoon. Sometimes we would visit the Heath where Rex sailed his boat upon the pond with intense concentration and glee, dogs barked and donkeys trotted up and down giving small people an occasional ride. On other days we would be taken for a walk whose peculiar quality remains in my memory till this day.

Somewhere off the Finchley Road there was a small footpath which culminated in what seemed to be a most perilously dangerous footbridge. It was a veritable Bridge of San Luis Rey. It was about a yard wide and suspended as far as the eye could see, high above an endless array of railway lines. The sides of this flimsy structure were trellised with wire, while beneath one's feet were ill-fitting boards, through which one could spy the perilous drop below. On each side shone this broad silver sweep of lines vanishing into the distance beyond both horizons. To me it was as if we were suspended in eternity. As we trod the flailing planks, we seemed hung between earth and sky, and the shining track sped away from us upon all sides, producing the effect of a glistening river speeding into infinity.

Present-day psychologists would no doubt deduce from this slight experience a 'conditioned reflex' in me thereafter, a predisposition, because of the fascination of those shining tracks, to dwell upon the concept of infinity. But as I understand it, the reverse is the way of it. On those afternoon walks, which did take on for me an inexplicable and thrilling significance, it seems that I was prodded to perceive that shining pathway and kindle to it, seeing along the myriad polished rails the flow of eternity.

3

My father was that most mysterious and unexplained thing called 'on the Stock Exchange', and though in after years he used to say that he was 'too honest to make any money at it', he used to have a good deal of interest and gaiety out of those Edwardian years of his early married life.

His parents lived in Kensington. My father was the youngest of five sons, none of whom had been trained for any particular profession. My grandfather was a prosperous wool trader and he had married the daughter of a china tea merchant, whose family

CHILDHOOD AND YOUTH

had made many intrepid journeys in the Tea Clippers to the China Seas.

My grandmother, Clara Moul, had died soon after I was born, but I still have a portrait of her in billowing taffeta and ostrich feathers, bound for the Court of Queen Victoria. With pardonable duplicity she was made to stand upon a stool within the folds of the voluminous gown, to give her little figure added stature.

Clara Moul married my grandfather Mead in about 1860. He, from his portraits, appears a trifle pompous and dull, decked in the paraphernalia of a Grand Master of his Masonic Lodge. But she, according to my father, was brilliant, intelligent and kind. My father was much indulged as the youngest son, and after he had followed his brothers to Marlborough College, instead of moving on to university, he was sent, because of his none too robust health, to Switzerland for two years. There, at a tutor's by Lake Geneva, he indulged to the full his love of life, of languages, of sport and of pretty girls. He won, as always at school and thereafter until the last year of his long life, many trophies for every kind of sport. But when he returned home, his trunks stuffed with silver cups and medals, it was realized with mild surprise that neither these nor his excellent French and German qualified him for any lucrative career. Thereafter he studied accountancy, faintly and with little interest, but more especially and with greater enthusiasm, the ploys of the English folk who, along with his parents, visited Homburg and the other fashionable German spas each summer.

But still his parents murmured, 'What is to be done with Frank?'

Even the doubtful honour of finding himself sharing a seat in a German park with Kaiser Wilhelm II and Edward, later to be the seventh king of that name, and overhearing the latter say to the former, 'She's a very vindictive woman!', did not equip him for any promising profession.

My grandparents had a great fondness for the stage, and for stage folk as well. Many of them came to their Kensington home for dinner parties and other social occasions, and my father grew up with a passion for the stage. George Grossmith Senior assured my grandmother that she would do well to let Frank take to the stage as a career, but she, perversely and with her drawing room filled with actors and actresses, retorted that it 'would break her heart'.

Charles Hawtrey, Ellen Terry, Cyril Maude and Ellaline Terriss (whose melodious speaking voice my father never forgot), Johnnie Toule and many others who met at my grandparents' house, whetted my father's appetite for this glamorous career, but it was not to be. Frank was put on the Stock Exchange as being more respectable. He was forced to content himself thereafter with only amateur acting and producing, which nevertheless delighted him until he was well over seventy years of age. A portrait of him as a schoolboy was painted by a friend, and as my father used to tell, 'when old Frith (of Derby Day fame) visited us one day, he looked at the portrait and said, "I painted that!"' And when my father explained that it was not him but his son who had painted it, Frith had growled, 'H'm, 's good nevertheless'.

Honesty, or ineptitude at making money – history does not relate the reason – led to my father's life, after so gilded a youth, being often clouded by financial cares. His father on his death should have left his family the bulk of his fortune, but (perhaps to do honour to his Lodge, as his sons averred) this went to charity, and the five sons had to be content with what they looked on as a minimal sum each. It was evidently supposed that 'they should by now be able to look after themselves'.

In those days the house party was the thing, and friends of my parents used to take for some months of the summer a mansion in the Thames Valley, to which their many acquaintances were invited.

I remember my father saying that these visits cost him in tips for the multitudinous staff nearly as much as a holiday in a good hotel – but no doubt this was an exaggeration. Ware, Fawley Court and others of the fine houses whose resplendent gardens sloped down to the peaceful waters of the Thames, were the scenes of the innocent – or not so innocent – enjoyments of my parents and their associates. In white flannels and straw boater my father would display his skill at punting. Or in navy blue stockingette bathing suit to the knees, with white stripes circling his athletic form, he would streak through the air in a swallow dive off the top of the boat house, while my mother shut her eyes as she 'never could bear to watch Frank dive from such dizzy heights'.

Occasionally we children were taken for brief visits to these house parties. I well remember the alarming old Lady Hanson, still modelled patriotically upon the long dead Queen Victoria, whose style had set seal upon half a century of English womanhood. She sat enthroned at the head of the long luncheon table, her hair strained away from the broad white parting and twisted firmly into a tight knot at the back of her head. Her pallid and remote countenance was framed by two broad hooped 'George Robey' eyebrows which my father said were painted with burnt cork. Her stiffly boned corsage was adorned with ropes of pearls, and bones supported the high net collar around her throat. Her personal maid was beside her, armed with a fly switch, for she had a terror of wasps, and the open windows in the rooms which she used were sealed with gauze frames.

Friends, fly switches still in evidence, accompanied her – now heavily veiled – upon the river picnics to which we all proceeded each afternoon, when one or two private launches, well-stocked with picnic baskets, conveyed us sedately under their striped awnings up the river, through flower-decked locks and between the buttercup fields of the mild Thames Valley. Enthralled, I would watch the sedgy river banks with fascination, where water rats scurried secretly away from the wash of the launch, and canopies of June roses hung down over the water.

These very amiable house parties continued until the outbreak of war in 1914 claimed the chauffeur, butler, footmen, boatmen, gardeners and other staff for the less smiling countryside of France under trench warfare . . . and the stately houses no doubt for hospitals and military HQs.

4

My mother's family lived at Heathside, an ivy-hung Regency house in Canon Place, Hampstead. My grandfather, Augustus Hounsham, when a little boy, had been taken by his parents to South America. History does not relate the purpose of this visit, but at the age of eight he was suddenly orphaned in that distant land when both parents were smitten with yellow fever and died within a few days of one another. Another relative sailed out to fetch him back, and she, too, died of the same disease. Augustus was taken to the British Consul who advertised for 'next of kin'.

At last an uncle succeeded in getting the child home and brought him up with his own children.

I never knew this grandfather either, but according to his photographs and my mother's account of him he was handsome, gay and loving to his family to the point of over-indulgence. He had crisply waving fair hair and a dashing beard, and he sang to the guitar in a way that enchanted his three daughters. He gave up his study so that the girls could turn it into an office for their production of the *Scribblers' Magazine*, of which my mother, as eldest, was editor. The staff of the *Scribblers* littered their father's room with their articles, paintings, drawings and the various literary gestures of their school friends. The magazine flourished for some years and was circulated in dog-eared copybooks. I had a pile of them until a few years ago, but alas, now they have disappeared.

When that grandfather died, which was while the girls were in their teens, my grandmother moved to Pangbourne on the beloved river Thames, to a cottage which the three girls had owned and used for holidays, while their friends stayed on houseboats nearby. This flower-clad thatched cottage still braves the banks of the limpid Thames, while instead of carriage and pair or a few intrepid cyclists in straw hats and bloomers, motor coaches, lorries and all the rest of the noisy flotillas of our day dash past its rose-twined windows, filling the quiet rooms with fumes and a ceaseless roar, while outboard motors and cabin cruisers add their cacophony to destroy the natural peace of the water meadows.

From this vantage point that summer, while the girls entertained their boy cousins and friends in punt and houseboat, my grandmother went off to find another home. The place she lighted on provided for us children a holiday paradise for many years to come.

The house she bought was in Wallingford, a little way up stream.

Stonehall was built upon the site of a thirteenth-century monastery, and after the Dissolution its structure was made from those ancient stones. (Incidentally, our Stonehall still stands where it always did, but by some quirk its name has been changed to Flint House and Flint Cottage, while the Georgian house next door has inexplicably purloined our name.)

CHILDHOOD AND YOUTH

Opposite the old house, across the road, lies the Kine Croft. In my unconscious way of separating the things around me into dark and light, I thought that this was the '*Kind* Croft'. It must be kind, for was not the Bull Croft over the high old garden wall at the back of the house? The Bull Croft was, of course, a dark and frightening place, though I never remember scaling the wall to dare its remoteness; but the name was forbidding enough to raise fearsome forebodings. There was a bull called 'Emperor' down by the river, and once he had chased my mother so that, flying along the towpath in her long skirts, she would have jumped into the water had not a passing punt taken her aboard. I had seen Emperor and heard his menacing bellow. So the Bull Croft was a place to be avoided while the Kine Croft was a smiling enclosure where we were safe. Indeed, it was filled with breath-taking romance, for round its flanks ran mysterious mounds where, we were told, lay buried the relics of armour and weapons from a fight between the Cavaliers and Roundheads. In actual fact, I have learned on a recent visit that the relics were of Saxon origin, but what matter such details? And it was 'Cavaliers and Roundheads' that we played over those mounds. To Stonehall went all the family for holidays. Just as nowadays the well-to-do escape the restless fume-laden atmosphere of London by fleeing to Bermuda or some South Sea Isle, and while in my adolescent years we went to Bembridge or Seaview in the Isle of Wight, so in those Edwardian and early Georgian days we went to 'the River'. It was the gentle playground of the Londoner. My father divided his holidays between Cowes, where he and his brothers sailed year after year, and the welcoming Thames.

My close comrade in those days was my cousin Phyl. She, Rex and I shared the joys of Stonehall in summer and Christmas holidays. Phyl was a little older than I, but in spite of her long legs and superior age we never had cause to notice this difference between us. She was fair haired – as I was – but she was a head taller and she sported two long pigtails that flew out behind her lissome figure as she ran. I was more solid, and always I found it hard, nay, impossible, to catch those two when we played hide-and-seek about the old house and garden.

Stonehall was dark, oak-panelled, with winding stairs and secret corners, yet none of those darknesses seemed gloomy to me. The whole house was pervaded by a warmth, a genial ambiance, a cosy security that I always felt and which lit all its corners as with a brazier's glow. As I grew older, I realized that this warmth, this fire which glowed through the whole house, was the radiation of my grandmother's warm heart. She died when I was fourteen, but I never heard any word from her or in her surroundings nor spoken of her, that had not the glow of a serene affection. She was mild, smiling and all things that were sweet to all people. I do not suppose that she was intellectual like her daughters, nor particularly clever. Her genius lay in the warmth of her loving disposition.

At holiday times Stonehall's hospitable walls needed to expand, for twelve or fourteen members of the family would descend upon it. Old Sarah Ives, or 'Ivy' as we children called her, was deputed to 'look after the children', and, of course, with such a party there must have been endless chores which my grandmother took upon herself. In summer it was a paradise for children from London. The ancient garden spread behind the house in lawn and flower beds flanked by tall yew hedges. Along one side ran a dim, mysterious yew walk which smelt of brandy snaps, for beyond the yews was a venerable malt house, now disused, whose pungent smell of hops permeated our games under its white-washed and crumbling walls. Beyond the lawn where lilac and snowball trees perfumed the air, through a curved archway in a clipped hedge, one entered the walled kitchen garden. Here the high old walls supported plum and peach trees, espalier-wise against the hot brick. We children had a tree each allotted to us, and there was competition as to whose fruits ripened first.

Here the paths were fringed with neat low-clipped box hedges, which, when you crushed them, gave off an aromatic fragrance that enveloped you as you lay against them, waiting to make a dash for 'home'. In this idyllic garden it always seemed to be summer. Golden rod and sunflowers reared high above one's head and you could creep in amongst their bee-thronged spears into a pollen-scented secret 'hide' of one's own.

The old stables, newly turned into modern usage as a garage, were cobbled, as was the courtyard outside. Moss grew between these mellowed stones which made it soft for small knees to fall on, and an old green water-butt stood in one corner. Within the stable reigned a resplendent thing . . . a real live motor car. It was of ochre yellow, and shone proudly with its brass lanterns and fittings. It was a rare and splendid creature, not lightly to be approached, and my thrill knew no bounds when my brother once suggested that we should hide from our pursuers under the tonneau cover. Naturally, no-one would ever dream of invading such sanctity, so snuggled up in the leather-smelling paunch of this wonderful monster, we giggled ecstatically until lunchtime.

My cousin Phyl was supposed to be growing too fast, and so, to rest her back, she was made to lie flat on the floor after lunch every day – in a room called 'the Den'. It was a peaceful sunlit place whose walls were hung with my aunt's – the youngest Hounsham girl's – competent water colours. Here, for a period of enchantment, my grandmother read to us 'The Secret Garden'.

To me, Stonehall and 'The Secret Garden', I suppose, are delicately intertwined. All the mystery, the wonder, the perfumes of other days, hang about my memory of each. Through that 'door in the wall' we merged with a mystery world, a place of bird song and honeysuckle, box and yew, towering phlox, and the bloom on a Victoria plum against a hot wall, which, when you pressed it, left a patch of shining purple on the velvet skin.

A garden such as this, either at a real Stonehall, or in the dream fantasy of that magic book, leads a child towards truth, towards a reality which is timeless in space, timeless in the memory, and it breathes of other worlds in other dimensions that one has known . . . one cannot remember where or when.

6

At that age I was, as one of my aunts later told me, 'impossibly squeamish'. I howled all too easily. As she said, 'One only had to say that Little Bo Peep had lost her sheep and there were prompt tears. It was of no use to explain that it was only a story. You howled for those wretched sheep!'

I see this now as a repercussion of a secret and shaking experience that sometimes would overtake me as a very small child. I would suddenly find myself fully awake in the darkness of the night, while through my head would be running the verses of a poem which must have been read to me at that time. It was 'The Lost Doll' by Charles Kingsley:

> 'I lost my poor little doll, dears,
> Out on the Heath one day. . . .'

The Heath, of course, must be Hampstead Heath. It was all true. And when the doll was finally found it was small relief, for its waxen face was all crushed and melted, its clothes all stained with mire. Some fearful thing had befallen it. And I would lie, melted and dissolved in an agony of pity for that unfortunate scrap. This recurred often enough to have a reason. And from the perspective of time I see it as a prompting from the Beyond to look on all hurt with sympathy. Perhaps I needed this lesson.

As I grew out of infancy my mother taught us little prayers. I kneeled upon the bathroom chair, face supposedly buried in newly dried hands. But as I said the words: 'Gentle Jesus, meek and mild, look upon a little child . . .' I keeked through my fingers at the jolly blue and white Dutch boys and girls upon the steamy tiled wall and these were prayer for me.

By the time I was seven we moved to Surrey. But this was not before I had seen my first pantomime. This involved a ride in a hansom cab. On shopping excursions with my mother hitherto I begged her to let that alarming monster, the new red motor bus, pass by, so that we could ride in the old horse omnibus which trundled comfortably along behind. The steaming bodies of the warm, patient horses, the smell of ordure, the creak and jingle of harness and the muffled clop of hooves spread a friendly aroma about the streets in those days, and the glimpse of a dray drawn up by a drinking fountain, or the milkman's pony with his drooping head thrust into his feeding bag, these were the sounds and sights which warmed the atmosphere of London at that time.

The trip in the hansom cab was a thing to be remembered. The brisk delight of its swift jolting motion through the brightly lighted streets, the horse's withers lilting in front of you, a light rain upon your face, and the surprise of the little trap door over your head as the cabby peered down for directions, the dash through the confusion of horse traffic all around . . . who would exchange these for the dead weight of our present day mêlée?

It is to be supposed that our seats at the pantomime were somewhere near the back of the dress or upper circle, for Drury Lane to me was a vast black velvet tunnel at the distant end of which was a small bright patch – and upon this people moved and sang. I could not at all follow what it was all about. Enveloped in that darkness and gazing at that distant oblong of light below, I was suddenly conscious of myself as being suspended apart from all this dense mystery and noise. Reality took a sudden spasm (which I grew accustomed to in future times) and I viewed it as from an angle quite detached from the event. I was calm, warm, tranquil, watching as from another dimension, totally uninvolved with the confusion that was going on around me. Plainly I was too young to appreciate pantomime.

Chapter Two

HIGH ADVENTURING

1

The house my parents chose when we left Hampstead was upon the rural fringe of the nondescript town of Woking, nearly thirty miles out of London. The prosaic little house stood in a small garden on the edge of fields which in those days were innocent of houses, and stretched for some miles towards the Merrow Downs above Guildford. These fields were our playground for years to come.

The Croft was a sunny house, and though my mother, bereft of her girlhood's friends and the sociable life of Hampstead, confessed to have wept for days when first the family settled in, we children were more than delighted with the change. For here, close about us, there were lanes hung over with oaks, hazel woods and wild rhododendrons, and in those sandy banks we found birds' nests and warrens of rabbits, while squirrels bounced along their overhead highways. So for a while exploring became our passionate pastime.

My brother was soon caught up with a group of other boys in the neighbourhood, so I developed my own absorbing occupations. Opposite our house, at the entrance to a field, was a great white gate which hung somewhat high over the cart track which wound through it. This gate became my point of balance, as it were. Whenever I was at a loose end, with nothing special to do, I resorted to my gate. If you opened it and pulled it back as wide as it would go, it swung back high up over the sloping ground. A little push and you were soaring through the air in a long slow flight. This could be repeated over and over again without ever becoming wearisome. One became airborne.

By now I had a dog, a white terrier, a long-legged and lop-eared most beloved companion. While I sailed through the air on my winged gate, 'Jack' would penetrate the dense coppice nearby and race after real or imaginary prey. Or he and I together would rove the woods and fields of the peaceful unfrequented valley.

Opposite our garden a bosky lane straggled along the edge of the field and then climbed sharply up towards Hook Heath. This lane was the highway of my daily life, for when school had started, up it I went each morning, between its high sandy banks topped with hazel thickets. The bright new green of the leaves was translucent as clear water against the sky. Leaves that curled usually held a caterpillar, wrapped as in a silken hairy eiderdown, and these must be collected and reared at home in a caterpillar crèche. And oh, the miracle to watch the slow moves of the little creature in its transition from its green and arching form, through its dormant stage, huddled in its chrysalis, woven miraculously by itself out of materials found within itself, to that form of beauty, the yellow gauzy-winged butterfly. In those days they were not poison-sprayed out of existence.

2

My mother taught us the sweet Gospel story, and on Sunday afternoons while my parents slept in the sunny garden, or by a log fire on winter days, my brother and I trudged the mile or so along the heath to Sunday School. Here, as well as singing cheerful hymns, we learned the dimensions of the Temple in Jerusalem, 'made from the cedars of Lebanon,' and finally we made a model of this building in cardboard, a thing that evidently every child should know.

Here, too, we were given little pictures to take home with us, one every Sunday, to stick in an album. They were so small, these pictures, as to be not much bigger than a large postage stamp, yet they imparted a secret alchemy to my life. They depicted little scenes in the Old Testament stories, or enactments in the life of Jesus and His disciples. Here was Abraham with Isaac, obediently carrying his own funeral pyre. Here was Moses striking the rock and finding water. Here was Joseph, with his coat of many colours, and here was Jesus teaching the people by the Lake of Galilee. The scenes were vividly painted and most brilliantly coloured in gold and yellow, vermilion, green and blue; and to me they provided an approach to a sense of heaven itself. The album containing them lay by my bed, with a night-light for company, and to live in each picture caught one up into a shadowless and 'happy land' like the one we sang about at school. They gave form to that sense of trust that supported life at that time.

So it did not seem in any way surprising that sometimes when in bed at night 'Jesus' would come to me.

Suddenly, either in the brightness of a summer evening or in the glow of my night-light, there would be beside me a radiant Being who showed Himself, or gave of Himself would perhaps be a more accurate term, for a space of a few moments, and then disappear. This was not the figure of Jesus as in my pictures, in robe and beard. This was not man-formed at all. Nor was it form seen with the physical eyes, but with a kind of mental seeing. It was a sudden sense of an individual Presence which gave out a force of benign blessing. It was as much a knowing as a seeing, a sudden spreading of awareness that took in the knowledge of a Presence hitherto unseen. I knew that to achieve this knowing, this seeing that was not seeing, I must use a certain sort of mental effort. It needed an acceleration of the mind in order to become aware of what the physical eyes did not see, but the mind knew to be present. It was like switching on a power which caused the brain and mind to burn.

I called this celestial Visitor 'Jesus' because I had been taught of Him. I thought it was 'Jesus on His rounds', so to say. Presumably it happened to everyone, so there was no need to mention it to those around me. And this Presence made itself known to me occasionally throughout my childhood days, and sometimes when at boarding school later on, sleeping in a dormitory with other girls.

In spite of this comforting phenomenon, fears in the dark would sometimes attack me. Though the house was essentially of a friendly atmosphere, a vague uneasiness would occasionally pervade the thick blackness. But there was an antidote to this. These shadows could be banished pretty swiftly by singing. Every song and hymn learned at Sunday School or around our piano must be brought up as an armament against the terrors of the night. It was a magic that always worked. Gradually the ominous shadows would fade away and a warm security would fill the room. Yet in spite of this secret alchemy now and again a far worse terror would approach. Suddenly I would come face to face with eternity.

'If I were not here where would I be?'

'If there were no world, no earth, no people, where would life be, where would I be, where and what was for ever and ever?'

Staring into the very heart of this thought caused an endless void to open before me which made the consciousness rock with fear. Only in later years did I find expression of this fear given by another, by Pascal:

'*Le silence éternel des espace infinis, m'affraye.*'

On the brink of this abyss I would stare and tremble, and wrench myself back with those little songs and hymns. A little while . . . one more will do it. And as a lamp clears a space of brightness in a dark cavern, so gradually would the shadows fade and all would be serene once more.

One day this sense of eternal security spread into the world of out-of-doors and sunshine. I was wandering alone in the fields which bordered our lane. It was high summer and acres of marguerite daisies spread in a white waving sea about me. I must have been about seven or eight years old, for the flowers were up above my elbows. Sprays of red sorrel pierced the undulating whiteness, and tall biscuit-coloured grasses. Bees hummed from flower to flower.

I stood still and listened.

And suddenly one of those transcendent moments took me. The lake of flowers shimmered and all at once it was as if my mind and sense of being spread out like a mist to embrace these living things. I felt myself to be one with the life which pulsated within them, and each flower and grass and sorrel and bee was a part of my own being and I was living in and through them. I *was* them. There was a realm of consciousness which lay behind the outer appearance and of which I was a part. It was an ocean of shining peace.

3

School brought new interests, and above all, new friends.

My brother being older than I was, imported boys whose legs were consequently longer, so that when my cousin Phyl was not staying with us, I would wander off alone, contented with a house I had made in a tree.

Phyl and I used to spend long summer days at a friend's bathing pool, and here one day we shamelessly broke the 8th commandment. As we left the pool and made our way across the friend's rambling garden, wet bathing things under our arms and long hair dripping round our shoulders, we spied a tree of enormous red apples. Thirstily we looked at them and then at each other. In a minute the thing was done. The apple was shaken down and stowed away in a towel. But so enormous was it that even when we had left the orchard and run down our home lane, the apple was too large, too rare a thing to eat. What was to be done with it? We couldn't take it home. Questions would be asked. So we took it into the field, hacked a cavity in the hard golden bank of sand, and stuffed it in, filling up the hole and smoothing away all traces of the crime.

And there it remained. For all I know a splendid apple tree is even now growing out of that bank, legacy of that guilty episode.

Except for the shortage of food and particularly sweet things, the war did not affect us children very much, and we were far enough from London for air raids not to disturb our nights. Only once did our parents wake to an unusual sound. A heavy rumbling was passing overhead of a kind that my father did not recognize. Getting out of bed, he went to the balcony. A giant Zeppelin was obscuring the sky.

He called to my mother, 'There's a Zeppelin overhead!'

My mother was unshaken, 'Wake me if anything interesting happens!' she murmured, and went off to sleep again.

And the massive dirigible grumbled its way over our fields towards Guildford and unloaded its bombs some six miles away. We children, of course, had heard nothing, being fast asleep.

It was about that time that my mother had a strange experience.

My father was staying away somewhere, and she heard that he was ill. She went to bed anxious about him. In the night she woke up stark awake, and got up out of bed. She had 'Frank' on her mind and she crossed the room thinking to get dressed and go to him. Then, chancing to look down at the bed, she was astonished to see her form still lying there asleep in the bed. She looked down at herself and found that she seemed as solid and real as usual, but she realized that she was out of her body. She paused in her determination. If she went to Frank in this state she knew that she would frighten him and perhaps increase his fever. She knew, somehow, that by an action of the will she could travel to him. But she hesitated, and then, with a concentrated act of will power, she forced herself back into her body again. Then she woke up normally with full memory of what had happened.

This type of occurrence took my mother by surprise several times during her life. She would not have it that she was psychic. She used to say, 'I don't believe in ghosts, but I am frightened of them!'

Her friends, the Balfours, at Fishers Hill near our home, were at this time deep in investigating the comparatively new science of psychical research. Living at Fishers Hill with Lady Betty Balfour and her husband Gerald (soon to inherit the peerage from his brother A. J. Balfour), were Mr Piddington and Mrs Sidgwick, celebrated names in the spiritualistic world of those days. But my parents, I think, had little to do with these activities of their friends, for I never heard them speak of it, though as children we went constantly to the house for parties and to perform Shakespeare on their spacious lawn.

However, when I grew older the story of my mother's curious experiences percolated through the family and I became accustomed to the idea that the essential soul should be regarded as separate from the physical body.

My parents at this time became intimate with a family who lived at the head of our lane. Edward White was a landscape architect of some international renown, a veritable Capability Brown, President of the Horticultural Society and founder of the Chelsea Flower Show. He was a bizarre character. He had an eighteenth-century elegance and manner and used a tall walking stick, as did Malvolio, as a gesture to elegance. Among his other gifts he was a considerable musician. Very soon he and his wife started to visit us often and each evening our house resounded with duets. My mother grasped at this opportunity to exercise her talent, and it was a thrill to me alone upstairs in bed, for by this time Rex had been dispatched to a preparatory school. Strains of Brahms, Beethoven, Mozart and other composers filled the house, and I would grow drowsy and fall asleep to the energetic playing of my elders.

Into this musical atmosphere, as time went on, there appeared a new friend on the scene, the celebrated composer, Dame Ethyl Smythe. At that time she was writing her opera, 'The Boatswain's Mate', and I remember her playing its themes on our piano and singing vociferously in her uninhibited and husky voice. I recall her singing the air of one of the songs in that opera, telling how the undertones of its theme had come to her on a Channel steamer – echoing the thrum of the engines – on her way home from abroad:

> 'Suppose you mean to do a given thing,
> And someone comes and says it's got to be done –
> Then all of a sudden you'd rather die than do it!'

My mother's life was thus gradually compensated for leaving London, and this was emphasized by the rising tide of calling cards which found their way into the silver salver in the hall, and the regular packet from the cleaners which lay by them so often, containing numerous pairs of long white kid gloves.

My father continued on the Stock Exchange for a while, travelling by train to London every day, until a wartime assignment led him to Farnborough, where he interested himself in aircraft designing. Money in those lean years was scarce, and finally the sole survivor of the staff who ran our house before the war was Aldy, now promoted from nurse to 'cook general'. Aldy, with her sudden gusty squalls of fierce temper, was a faithful true-hearted prop to the family. She would spend hours singing to me in the kitchen while she ironed or made pastry. She had a touching adoration for my mother and called her 'Glory'. She stayed with us for thirteen years.

My mother took up photography as a hobby and a kind of war work. She studied portraiture in London with Hugh Cecil and Compton Collier (well-known names in that field at the time), and soon was using her innovation of taking her camera to the homes of men about to leave for the Front. As well, she photographed Edward White's superlative gardens for the Duke of Connaught and many other gardens of the great.

With Lady Betty Balfour, ever an earnest social worker, my mother organized 'the Kitchener Club' for the soldiers, running the musical entertainments, training the orchestra and giving many concerts herself, either playing the piano or conducting. And so gradually our drawing room filled with soldiers rehearsing their instruments, either in twos and threes or in full orchestra. My mother was fulfilled at this time. Hers was an intellectual as well as an ardently warm and enthusiastic temperament, and unless her energies were fully engaged, though she tried to fill her time with much reading, she was unsatisfied. I was to see the results of this in later years.

Two episodes in her girlhood illustrate her uninhibited character.

She confessed that as a girl she had been envious of her sister's bright colouring, and as make-up in those days was unheard of among the well-brought-up, she hit upon an ingenious device. Her large bound volume of Shakespeare was a pinkish colour. Before going to a dance where she longed to look her most engaging, this sedate volume was carefully sponged and the enviable pink transferred to my mother's pale cheeks. When this book came to me I used to wonder at its patchy and anaemic appearance.

On another occasion 'Clare' was on her way to a garden-party, elegant in her gown of lace and frills, with a wide tea-ed up picture hat. The day looked threatening, so reluctantly she took an umbrella with her. As she neared her objective the clouds faded away and the sun shone steadily. The large black umbrella must not be allowed to spoil the effect of her fastidious get-up. She cast about for a solution. Impulsively prancing into the middle of the road, she thrust upon an astonished crossing-sweeper the gift of an excellent umbrella.

My parents and Dame Ethyl Smythe were near neighbours and saw a good deal of one another, and many were the amusing tales that percolated down to me of her eccentricities. Endless anecdotes tempt the pen. On one occasion when my parents were at a concert that Dame Ethyl was conducting of her own works, she stopped the orchestra in mid-flight and broke in with the words, 'That passage is so beautiful, let's have it again!'

As is well known, she was a close friend of that figure which looms from history to be linked with this era, the Empress Eugenie, widow of Napoleon III, who lived in retirement not far away on the Farnborough Hills. Dame Ethyl, eccentric in costume as well as behaviour, dressed till her end in a suit of masculine cut, surely tailored in the Victorian century, stiff collar and Homburg hat. She would ride to Farnborough on her bicycle, and she told how the Empress used to post someone in the hall 'to tidy up Ethyl when she arrived'.

I well remember her coming to our house one day during the Kaiser's war and crying, 'Guess what I've got on underneath!' And throwing her long skirts over her head, she disclosed to the startled gaze of the mixed company a pair of land girl's breeches.

My mother found much stimulation in Dame Ethyl's company and I well remember when I was in my teens her shouting over the heads of the occupants of the local bus, 'The most intelligent woman in Woking, your mother!'

4

It was natural that this strong tide of adult life which was flowing through the house should sweep an insignificant child into the backwaters. Many are the evenings that I spent in the kitchen with Aldy where I was put to polishing the old-fashioned jelly moulds of copper in the quaint shapes of fishes and hearts and seashells which adorned the dresser, gleaming in the glow of the kitchen range. When a telegram came for Aldy one day, with the news that her brother had gone down with his ship off Gallipoli, Aldy put her apron over her head and howled, while I sententiously told her that she should not cry as her brother 'would be far happier in heaven'.

But often Aldy was too busy to bother with me, so much of my day was spent with my animals. But these did not always spell happiness. All too often death removed them foully and irrevocably. My father gave me pigeons, but the dogs and cats were too much for them. A heap of tangled feathers was sometimes all I could find. I had white mice housed in an old doll's house, and even their way of producing every so often half a dozen more of their kind, could not keep up with the mortality rate from the predatory cats. Guinea pigs and rabbits sometimes suffered the same fate, till at last my mother, to salve my tears, cried, 'You shall have a goat, you shall have a kid!' Frantically she named the first animal that came into her head, which seemed too big to fall a prey to natural events.

HIGH ADVENTURING

So a six weeks' old kid was found for me, the most amiable little creature, which my father named 'Vimy' after the battle now raging in France – whose gunfire on still days we could hear dully, over the Surrey hills.

Vimy became a dearly loved friend and he, with Jack the terrier, went everywhere with me. So for a while my mother's ingenuity defeated the threats of nature red in tooth and claw.

Bordering the winding green tunnel which led up to Hook Heath and school, there was a garden which became my private treasure . . . private, that is, only until I found a school friend to share it with. It was a long straggling garden of an acre or two, hedged in places with wild rhododendrons. The house stood some way back from the belt of beeches which surmounted the deep banks along its boundary to the south, and was invisible from my trespassing eyes. But I knew it had stood empty for some little while.

Fernhill became an object lesson in living. It showed me early that secret longings have a way of coming true. For I longed that we should live there.

At the bottom of the steep orchard that fringed one side of this 'promised land' stood a wooden door, firmly fastened with a Yale lock. But by creeping through a gap in the rhododendron hedge I and my animals found a way in. Uncertain whether gardeners might be about, I stalked with fluttering heart up the steep orchard path to reconnoitre. No one appeared, so I pressed on. It was spring time and the orchard was decked with apple blossom, plum and pear; cellandines spread a carpet of glossy gold among the rough tussocky grass, and clusters of narcissi, white winged, were near to my appreciative nostrils as I climbed the steep mounded hillside under the leaning fruit trees. Crowning the summit of the orchard stood a mighty cherry tree in full blossom, and from one of its powerful branches hung a swing. It was the swing of a child's dream. Its ropes were firm and long, reaching right up into the whiteness above. Its seat was broad and inviting. It was in fact irresistible. Scrambling up into position and poised for flight, my toe only just touched the ground. A shove, a swing of the legs, and my chariot took wings. Out over the falling ground it soared, out into the fragrant air. With long slow majestic sweeps it carried me back and forth, up into the blossom overhead and then out over the narcissus strewn slope.

Here was a new freedom, a new dimension.

Gradually the technique developed. One must swing as high and as far out as could be, and then at the peak of the long outward flight, one must leave go and leap, flying through the air and landing in a rolling tumble on the soft long grass.

This was a thrill to be shared, and I soon brought my special school-friend K. to join me in this paradise.

The rhododendrons and azaleas had finished flowering, the cherries ripened while the brown squirrels nibbled their juicy fruits and disdainfully cast their stones down upon our heads below, the beeches had turned golden and the apples were rotting in the long grass, and then suddenly Fernhill was ours . . . ours, our very own.

The family moved into Fernhill when I was twelve, the Sion of my dreams.

5

Fernhill was a largish house of commodious early Victorian design. It was set upon high ground with its lofty rooms filled with sunshine. The sloping lawns fell away from the front of the house, where stood a splendid cedar tree. My room faced out to the Merrow Downs, and Vimy was contentedly snug in the hay loft of the stables at the end of the drive.

With my mother's increased preoccupation with her photography and musical activities, my world was the garden, the animals and school. This was a small private school nearby, run by two learned sisters, the Misses Rogers. They must have been excellent teachers, for work seemed interesting and simple. I took a satisfactory number of prizes while at that school. It was not till the age of fourteen, when I was sent to boarding school, that I slumped to near the bottom of the form, and this was because I found life more interesting than work.

One point I recall, because it was so frequently remarked upon. The mistresses would constantly reproach me for putting the palm of my hand to my forehead. Had I a headache? Was I not feeling well?

I was feeling perfectly well, but often, and all through my life, I became accustomed to the sensation of a burning in the centre of my forehead which was cooled by placing a palm upon it.

From the time I was very young, long before I had learned to read, the idea had somehow got into my family that 'C. adores books and is going to be an author'.

True it was that as time went on I did adore books, even the feel and look of them, but as for being an author, there was very little sign of that. At school my performance was very mediocre. But reading was all absorbing, a world in itself, especially books about certain past centuries. Sometimes the intensity with which the sense of actually *being* in certain periods took me by surprise. It was as if I knew it all, had lived in that time, could smell the ethos of those days, the pain, the fear, the love. But it was many years before a type of 'seeing' began to develop which might be called 'flashbacks', in which one actually lived as though in a timeless state through those ancient happenings.

I was tall and well-developed for my age and became used to being taken for two or three years older than I really was. Perhaps it was for this reason that I had the good fortune sometimes to act in the school play the parts of Portia and others.

Kipling said that 'smells are surer than sounds or sights to make the heart-strings crack'. And the aroma of Portia had that effect upon me. The Elizabethan language, the costumes, the corded silk doublets, the rich velvet gowns, the hose, the head-dresses, the music, the galliards danced, these somehow became impregnated with the heady perfume of syringa, for we acted in the garden in high summer, either at the school or in the garden of Fishers Hill, the lovely Lutyens house of the Balfour family. Swimming in that Elizabethan atmosphere inexplicably set the lute string of memory vibrating nostalgically in a way that was utterly puzzling:

'It made my heart-strings crack . . .
It started that awful whisper o' nights . . . come back, come back.'

6

Small events set up new trains of thought.

One day I was by our stream, alone but for Jack, who, wallowing in the water in between his sallies after rabbits, was scattering the tadpoles I had gone there to collect. A group of cows munched buttercups nearby.

My jar was soon filled with the wriggling creatures, some as round as pellets, some with embryo legs protruding adventurously from their disappearing tails.

A frog was among them. I extracted him and sat him on my hand. He watched me, his throat gulping, clutching my finger with his hand.

I examined him attentively. His arm and shoulder, his elbow and his tiny hand were ridiculously like my own. He even had a thumb and fingers such as mine.

If we were made in the likeness of God, were frogs then made in His likeness too?

How could this be?

Was not God maker of Earth and stars and sky? Was He not spread through the Empyrean behind all things? What use had He for arms and legs and hands? And how could He transfer these likenesses of Himself to this frog – and to me?

I put the frog back in the water, and calling Jack wandered across the yellow carpeted field. The day was hot, so I sat down in the shade of an oak tree which grew by the dry, dusty bank.

The roots of the oak protruded out through the soil and spread over the surface near me. I had been paddling and now I kicked off my sandals and sunned my bare feet.

I stared at my toes.

They were strangely like the frog's.

I leaned against the welcoming angle of the oak tree's sprawling roots.

Why, the oak had feet and toes as well! Just look how that root splayed out into smaller limbs! And its spine reared up straight like mine; its arms that spread out over my head ended in finger-like twigs.

I lay on my back and looked at the sky, with its white clouds foaming against the blue.

A rook whirled slowly, planing on the wind. And then I noticed that its wings were tapered at the ends into the semblance of fingers. The great spread of wing was like an arm clothed in feathers and at each extremity were finger-like extensions, five of them.

Why had I not noticed this before?

After that I became more observant and wherever I looked I

found examples of this astonishing similarity of make-up in all nature. The same ground plan pervaded so many things. At school I asked the botany mistress. Had she noticed? Why was this? She could proffer no satisfactory answer. She supposed it was God's plan, she said. With this vague explanation I was not at all satisfied. I thought it did not explain the likeness of things one to the other. On the heath I found a spray of dried bracken. It had a spine and ribs like my own.

7

It is not my plan to write fully of my life in its outward details, but merely to show some of the formative experiences which carried me along at that time.

When I left school I was sent to a college daily, where I studied drawing, music, languages and psychology. I still read voraciously. Plainly Pope was right. The proper study of mankind was man. That was the heyday of the first-rate novelist. The writer whose assessment of men and women is 'psychologically sound' is a teacher of life in his own right. He 'holds up a mirror to nature' for all to study. So it was plain that one could extend one's vision and live a broader life by proxy. I read Somerset Maugham, Hugh Walpole, Hitchens and the Bensons, Philip Gibbs and Ernest Raymond, Rosamond Lehmann, Galsworthy, Storm Jameson, Virginia Woolf, Arnold Bennett, Wells and Hugh Williamson. There seemed to be an unlimited range of 'worlds' to live in, in which one could savour life on a broader base than one's own limited horizon.

When I was eighteen, a friend offered me a job in his office in London. This was in the Society for the Promotion of Christian Knowledge, and of course I jumped at it, in spite of the scantiness of my secretarial training. I had not long returned from a period in France and was avid for larger doses of life with a capital 'L'.

It is to be confessed that only one tenth of my attention was on the job in SPCK House – for which I was paid 25s a week. In fact, being a very junior member of the staff, there was very little for me to do, and my friend the Manager, sensing my restlessness, often sent me out on invented errands. So I was free in the university of the world to dawdle through the streets with my eyes open. I haunted the picture galleries and second-hand book shops, and every penny I could muster went on the theatre and books. Bumpus yielded up some eye-openers. I found Samuel Butler's *Note Books*. Was he right when he said that 'Marriage must be immoral since the pleasure comes first and the pain afterwards'? Dunne's *Experiment with Time* set a new spark kindling. I read Jung and Freud, John B. Watson and Pavlov, William MacDougall and Crighton Miller. Our psychology lecturer had said that 'Genius is the perception of analogies'. From a certain angle this might be true, but it seemed that the genius which flamed from the canvases of Turner, Van Gogh, Fragonard, Canaletto, Michelangelo and a thousand others, was aglow with something more redolent of the Divine than this chill assessment. This same professor startled us by rejoicing that he 'no longer needed music'. He said that as a younger man he had found intense pleasure and release in music, but since he had, as it were, riddled the boiler of his subconscious, he was relieved to find that he no longer needed the 'opiate of music'.

The study of psychology contained the defects of its virtues. In one aspect it cleared the mind of the cobwebs of blind emotionalism and I welcomed its cleansing analytical methods. It often laid bare the motives for our irrational actions and speech. But through it I was brought temporarily to mistrust the inner knowing. I did not realize then that once we become dislocated from our own seat of judgement which is the Higher Self, we tend to wander lost in the mazes of human opinion. There the search can be endless.

A period of scepticism consequently closed down on me.

But gradually certain inner indications cleared the clouds away.

I remember particularly one such indication or signpost toward a renewed certainty in the Light within.

I was out in the fields again. After walking for a while I settled myself down against a high sandy bank in the warm sunshine. I had often rested at this spot before, but today there was something unusually magnetic in the atmosphere. The sand along the bank glowed golden and reflected the sunshine back into the tingling air. I sat alert, waiting and quiet. There was a sense of intensification of power around me. The light seemed to grow dazzling.

Then I heard the words, spoken not upon the ear but in the head. They came not as a sequence but as a phrase entire, as a die stamped into warm wax:

'Light is of God. Light *is* God.'

My dog came up panting and flopped down beside me. I stroked his silky ears. I reflected that I must have been dreaming. These were ordinary words which one had often read before. But somehow the impact was actual and deeply penetrating. I was certain that I had heard these words, and the impression remained strongly imprinted.

There came a time when my constant companion, Jack, died of a ripe old age. I was eighteen and he had been with me for twelve years. I was desolated and forced to think out the problem of death. To assume that the living flame of this vital creature was extinguished for ever was an offence against the Divine economy.

But the Church taught that animals had no souls.

Yet 'Not a sparrow falls to the ground but the Almighty knows of it'. But is He able to put out a hand to stay its fall?

Why was so much fear and suffering at the heart of life?

Why was nature 'red in tooth and claw', and why was man so savage in his dealings both with animals and with his own kind?

How could man survive the world's agonies? How, oh how could he be comforted?

As soon as I began to think, I found that sometimes a meticulous dispensation hung over my selection of books. If I was carrying with me a particular problem, some philosophical perplexity, quite certainly a book would present itself to me that would help my thought. It would literally be under my eye and hand as I roved the shelves. Sometimes it would even fall open at the very page whereon the problem that was itching me was discussed.

One day I came across in this manner a pair of volumes by Sir Arthur Conan Doyle. They were called *The New Revelation*, and for me they opened a window on to a new field of thought, a new world. They contained a simple introduction to the truth of 'Survival', the continuance of life as a natural process. Here it was not stated as a pious hope, a matter for faith alone. It was set forth as part of the laws of nature.

How sane, how clear, how logical.

I read Sir Oliver Lodge's *Raymond*, Myer's *Survival of Human Personality* and a number of other books on this enthralling subject.

It was an eye-opener of the first order and gave me what I needed. No need for tedious investigation of a practical kind. As I read I felt a deep inner certainty, irrefutable, incontrovertible.

These books spoke of animals too. This, then, was the wisdom behind nature. The soul of each living thing was eternal, sustaining itself in other realms of being. The body was left behind as an outworn coat no longer needed in other planes of subtler being.

I learned that when the soul went on it used a form, a finer body, yet duplicate of its physical form, suitable to the dimension it was inhabiting and its degree of awareness. I learned that human beings are recognizable to their friends when they meet in the next plane of existence, seeming as they did on Earth, though in full splendour of health and well-being. Thus it was that the cloud of sorrow for the world lifted somewhat and the air grew lighter.

However, I reflected that it was strange that the churches have been telling us this for centuries, but we still consider death the worst of tragedies. Does no one really believe the heart of the Christian teaching?

In my reading upon the subject of 'Survival' I learned of guides and teachers who made it their duty and their joy to help those left behind in the fogs of Earth. They taught of the continuity of life – to those who would listen.

These then were the saints who had gone ahead, to whom the Catholic Church prayed.

Then a thought struck me. The celestial Visitor who had come to me from time to time as a known but unseen Presence (seen only with the eyes of the mind), surely he might be such a one?

The words which occasionally hit upon my inner ear – What were these? Whence came they? It was impossible, absurdly presumptuous to think that I was hearing 'the Voice of God'. Might not these words have come from such a guide, such a teacher?

At that time I chanced to be staying in Sussex, and one day I walked out alone upon the downs above Birling Gap. The air was brilliant and salt-tanged, a lark trilled high overhead and as I walked my feet disturbed the bright flowers of the stonecrop and thyme and set free their fragrance. There was only the sound of the skylark and the distant thud of the breakers on the rocks below. My spirits, keyed to the serenity of the great silent expanses of biscuit-coloured downland, lifted and soared with the lark. I bounced along the springing turf, inhaling the sparkling air and feeling that I could fly.

Suddenly the now familiar change took place. The physical focus of the mind slipped from its entanglement with the senses. Like a balloon filled with hydrogen, my point of focus lifted and winged away into a spiritual dimension far from the level of life around me. Joy caught at me and tossed my spirits sky-high. I laughed and ran – anything to liberate the exalted tension within – and my awareness vaulted over the obstacles of mere seeing and hearing and erupted onto a plane of experiencing-by-being. Here the light was white, blaze-pure and splendid with the stuff of hope.

I knew that I had touched and savoured truth, a reality of being beyond the illusion of form and matter. This splendour which lies eternally behind the mists of human thought is the essence of the Universe; it is ever waiting to spill its joy into us and brim us with its fiery sweetness, its tonic force. Neither human frailties, nor fortune, nor earthly joys could contribute to it one gasp of delight nor take from it a fraction of its platinum worth. It was the stuff of Spirit, the light of the world . . . and there for everyone's taking.

Chapter Three

AWAKENING

1

I grew up, I travelled a good deal, living in Berlin through those days when Hitler rose to power, I married and 'lived happily ever after'. I had a son. Upon none of these events need I dilate, important though they are to me. I wish merely to chronicle the stepping-stones, those spiritual experiences which extended the awareness somewhat.

It was on a grey day in November 1934 that something happened which changed the focus of my life.

I was sitting relaxed and thinking.

Suddenly a colossal power filled the room, flooding it with golden light. Tension trembled round the walls. My consciousness ignited to a sudden flame. A permeating Presence filled the room, not gentle, acquiescent, tender as had been my childhood vision, but wholly compelling, purposeful, demanding.

I crossed to the window and looking out saw the trees transfigured into flames, and knew that my awareness had in some way changed. During those past days of scepticism it had often appeared to me that trees, perhaps more than any other natural thing, took on in some way the static quality of a stage backdrop. Now I saw that they and every other thing had caught fire. The very curtains of the room were iridescent with a vibrating life of their own. My eyes were opened and I was seeing things as they are, a mass of whirling energies filled with light.

I felt that I too was on fire, and it was a fire radiant with life.

When the exaltation had abated somewhat, I hurried out to the village and bought a pocket edition of the New Testament. I would study it again. Here, surely, I would find explanation of that which had struck me as lightning cleaves a tree.

So I began to think afresh, exploring as I went the inner regions of the mind. This practice, as I afterwards learned, was called 'Meditation', or in the East 'Yoga', though at the time I did not think of it in that way. In this search into the multiple dimensions of the consciousness, my earlier study of modern psychology steadied me, and warned me of the divers dangers and pitfalls on the way of this seeking. I knew that only through one's own experience could one learn, and so I set out to find the way.

Whenever I could, I practised. Sometimes for several hours a day it was my thrilling occupation. I hacked away at the slippery slopes of the glass mountain of consciousness, finding it as exasperating and as difficult as any hard-learned technical pursuit. Yet always I felt at the back of me a compulsion urging me on.

Development was not quick. Often I despaired of getting any further towards – I knew not what. I noticed that whenever I sat quietly, or lay down to sleep, in a few moments it would seem as though my head were filled with light, and it was this light which I sought to pierce. If it were night time I would often start up, thinking that I had left the light on by my bed. But no, with eyes open all was dark. Close the eyes again, and the light would flash forth. This made it difficult to sleep at night, and so when busy days did not permit very long at this inner practice, I would lie awake for many hours struggling to find out what went on inside my head.

It was an exciting quest. I was buoyed up with the hope, the certainty in those lines of Rupert Brooke which had haunted my girlhood: 'I shall find soon in the silence the hidden key to all that had hurt and puzzled me....'

I took with me into that silence the words: 'Be still and know that I am God.' And it was this stillness that I strove to achieve.

I found that – for the daytime – there was a technique of posture. One should be upright though relaxed and in comfort, with the base of the spine touching the back of the chair. A curved spine seemed to block the inrush, the uprush of power.

As time went on things began to happen. It seemed that a skylight in the top of the head began to open and I came out into a place of light. Within the varying levels of consciousness, slowly I was finding my way. It seemed to me that pressure of the mind and will, effort and ardour were the factors which raised the mental focus. I came to think of the mind as the operator of a lift; more power, greater height. I began to recognize the stages of the ascending scale. The consciousness was like a skyscraper, storey upon storey. More pressure exerted, the use of more power brought about the acceleration of the mind's energies and up would fly the lift of one's conscious awareness. Taking this analogy of the skyscraper, we can think of the varying layers of mental awareness as the rising storeys. The first floor was the first stage of abstraction. The next was the level of sleep. One must avoid lingering here, remaining watchfully alert, or one would doze off to wake later with all one's precious spare time gone.

Interest is the sharpener of all effort – interest and a sense of ardency, joy and high adventure. These accelerated the ascent.

One must exercise ceaseless vigilance. Every depression or acceleration must be observed in order to keep direction. It seemed that the focus of consciousness was as a miner's lamp strapped to the forehead, lighting the way along dark tunnels and shafts. The tunnels often were dead ends, while the shafts led upwards and must be followed.

There were always aids along the path which made me feel that I was not alone. One night I awoke sharply and sat up. Beside my bed in the darkness hung a gauzy veil. It was made of light and was, I judged, about six feet high and wide. In the centre of the lacy mesh was a great rent. As I gazed the apparition slowly faded until all was dark again, but there were words ringing in my ears: 'The veil between the worlds shall melt.'

Another night I saw in the darkness a silver landscape. This became the hallmark of a certain standard arrived at. The landscape was made of light and of such brilliance that it burned the mind to look at it. When I closed my eyes, even to remember, the vision seered and hurt. I came to use it as an exercise. I knew it had been given me to use as such. If I could hold that blinding memory then I was making progress. Gradually I trained myself to hold it for lengthening periods. It came to represent a high marking on the spiritual dial. Once I awoke thirsty and rose to fetch some water. As I crossed the dark room I saw that my person was luminous, phosphorescent like a glow-worm. Yet even as I stared the luminosity faded.

AWAKENING

As time went on I took to thinking questions into the centre of that light which was reached in meditation, and I found that answers were percolating into my mind. Vital experiences in inner planes were teaching me, as well as words. Disturbances in the outer world, threats of war and constant reminders of a world filled with tragedy – as reflected in the newspapers and wireless – heightened an eagerness to understand, a longing to mitigate, to comfort the universal cry of anguish.

Then one day, after years of concentrated effort, it seemed that a stage had been arrived at wherein one was enabled to accept the light. Suddenly it was as if a shaft of steely light penetrated and suffused my being. It pierced, irradiated and burned away both body and consciousness, leaving only a flame in the place where I had been. In this was agony as well as bliss. It held and tore at the vital core of my being and held me in its power – sometimes for what seemed a long time. In it was a sweetness, an ecstasy beyond description, and a kind of death as well. Often it came to me, over a period of several years. It was hard to extricate oneself from that compelling pain. The fire suffused one's being day and night and all one's working day must be got through while some degree of this ecstasy lasted. It was as though a white fire held me like an incense or an electrocution.

And in this state my prayer expanded into a kind of knowing.

I knew that God is indeed all light, and that all light, from that of a candle up to the sun and beyond, is in its degree expression of the Divine. Physical light is a reflection of that Light Beyond which sheds its lustre through the Empyrean upon the inner planes of being. This scale of Reality exists, from dense matter up to the Infinity of Spiritual Powers, and of these latter are the heavens made. We are of Spirit in essence, and God is this as well. I saw that Him to whom we human beings pray, is not the Cause and Sustainer of all that is, but a localization of the Most High, a personalized Glory as is the sun amid the conflagration of the galaxies. Of the Ultimate we could know nothing; His beams are brought to us through Lesser Lights. I knew no name for That which I had found.

The light of the mind of a man is but the cool end of that shaft of Holy Lightning, the down-graded radiation of the Supreme Luminary. The fire that the human mind is able to develop through prayer and practice rises towards the fringe of the inner

Light which is of God: and this is the spume of That which is beyond description.

All from lowest to highest is one colossal Whole.

And what holds this Universal Conflagration together?

These words came into the silence of my mind: 'The Law of Love. It is the cohesive factor in all things.'

Chapter Four

NEW PATHS

1

In June 1939 Wystan and I had our usual inspiriting holiday in the Lake District, while Nicholas, our son, now five years old, stayed with Wystan's mother at the Vicarage in Hove. Yet when we were all home again and I watched Nicholas playing on the sands, the persistent thought seemed to be forced into my mind, 'Nicholas needs a change of air. Arrange a holiday in the West Country.' I thought this was foolish and unnecessarily extravagant. We lived on the easternmost tip of Kent and the air was very bracing there. But the idea persisted. It was almost speech that I heard, reiterating within me, 'Nicholas needs a change of air. Arrange a holiday in the West Country.'

I began to mention it to Wystan and went off to buy a copy of 'The Lady'. In the advertisement columns I found a notice of a farmhouse which took paying guests, near Langport in Somerset. I wrote and booked for the three of us from Saturday, September 3rd.

The news became more ominous.

When I married and joined my life with Wystan's I gave up my custom of diary writing, and Wystan took to etching our joint lives in a five-year diary. But the habit of thinking through a pen was too strong to set aside entirely, so I continued occasionally to dash off little sketches so as to catch for ever the happiness of the life of the three of us together, which seemed to me quite perfect.

Here is a fragment. It was 1937. Evidently our three-year-old Nicholas was very exercised about 'God'.

'I found him in the garden today, lying on the lawn pointing a camera up to the sky. "I am taking a photograph of God," he said. "I expect He will look out between the clouds. I suppose it will come out God?"

'As I pushed him along in the pram yesterday I was reciting Hiawatha as we went along. Suddenly he fired questions at me, "Does God have a chair to sit on in the clouds?" And, "I suppose God comes down and walks about like we do sometimes?"

'The other day we were out in the woods and he was frolicking like a young lamb, and he paused and said what fun it would be to go to heaven and have a body that won't get scratched and hurt on brambles. "And Muma would come along and see my old body lying there and say, 'That's no good any longer!' and take away the tea."

'And another time he said, "It's funny, when I look at you I don't really think you are there really, it is only my eyes that are there. Oh, when we get to heaven God will explain these things, how we see, how we speak, how we hear. We'll even ask the angels what it was like before there was God!"

'I said, "There never was a time when there was no God."

' "No," he answered, "without God there would be no us, no animals, no life, no world, no sun, no stars, no anything. If God withdrew himself from everything, the whole world would crumble." And, "We could not go to the topmost heaven, could we, because God is there. And He doesn't sit on a throne surrounded by riches. He is much too humble." And on the sands one day, watching a fish lying in his shrimping net, he said, "It is like Jesus dying on the Cross."

In 1939 he was five. I tried the experiment of taking him to church. It was a lovely summer's day and the church door stood open. We sat in the porch and listened while the people were singing. Then Nicholas said with resolution, "No. The music is too sad. You were wrong to bring me."

And there is a short description of a doting 'Muma' seeing her slim little son off to school on his proud new tricycle; pale blue jersey, long slim brown arms and legs, and a white linen hat like a convulvulus over his fair hair. His last turn to wave again before butting the school gate open with the tricycle wheel, a happy smile and he is gone. There are some things too sweet for tears.

Then one day we three came back from the sands in that hot summer to find a circular thrust through our letter box. It showed a child in a gas-mask dead upon the steps of its school. We were urged to read the Civil Defence regulations.

2

Later in that month we did a thing which was quite aside from our usual pattern. It was a hot, windless Sunday, and normally we would have packed a picnic lunch and taken Nicholas to the sands. But there was a strangeness in the air, and I suggested that we went inland 'to explore the river Stour'.

We left the car by an inn called 'The Dog and Duck' and set off to walk along the fields which boarded the sluggish river. The sun was baking and we looked for a shady place to rest.

A bend in the river disclosed a large white yacht moored alongside the tow path. As we came abreast of it a bizarre figure appeared in the companion way and hailed us. In a broken accent he offered us a row in his dinghy. We hesitated, so the stranger said, 'Perhaps the little fellow would like a row?'

He was fair haired and bearded, a stalwart figure, wearing a sailcloth-coloured artist's smock. At his friendly overtures Wystan went across the gangplank and together they untied the dinghy. Nicholas of course was excited. So we piled picnic things, dog and child into the boat and pulled away up stream, the stranger watching us. As we turned to wave we saw the words 'Never Mind' painted along the bows of the yacht.

This was the beginning of a deep friendship which lasts to this day. We were taken on board later, given coffee by Simon and his wife, and we found ourselves in immediate warm accord with these two. A strong tide of life flowed through them both and the four of us have been bound by a warm affection ever since. We visited them often and sat in the saloon of the yacht, sipping coffee made Dutch fashion, with salt and a little butter (for Simon was Dutch), and talking, discussing, arguing until late at night. And then they two would escort us back along the quiet river to the inn, and in those light summer nights we could see the rosebay willow-herb and meadow-sweet fringing the banks, and smell the heady fragrance. Simon was of a somewhat scientific attitude of mind, in spite of being an artist, and we found that Pippa had no specially fixed ideas about anything. She would exasperate us by arguing from one angle one day, and by the next she would have veered round to the opposite position. We would cry, 'But yesterday you said. . . .' 'Oh that was yesterday!' she would answer lightly. She was a gay and delightful personality, disarmingly frank, a warm and most affectionate friend.

The thunder clouds of war were rolling towards us, and those last days of uneasy peace were helped for us by the pleasure we took in our new friends. Simon developed asthma, and thinking it due to the misty river we fetched them to stay with us, and Simon painted Nicholas. While I read him the *Just So Stories* he sat with a faraway look in his eyes which Simon caught to perfection. He painted me as well, but the faraway look in my eye saw years of terrifying war ahead.

We lived then on the eastern-most coast of Thanet, with Manston airport a few miles away, and everybody expected immediate and devastating raids, should war come. We were booked for a holiday in Somerset and so with heavy hearts we began to pack. The impulse to book that holiday was prophetic to the very day. We stowed everything we could into the car. I secretly kissed the lintel of the door of the house that Wystan and I had built seven years before, a tear-blurred look at the garden we had made together and loved, and our new friends waved us goodbye.

We drove to my parents in Woking, persuaded my mother to accompany us into Somerset, and set off. Impossible to describe the leaden load in our hearts at that time. It was the same for everyone. As Chamberlain said: 'The lights of Europe are going out.'

We arrived at our lonely farmhouse of Aller Court on September 2nd. We found the farmer struggling with the unaccustomed task of blacking out. Candles lit the gaunt scene. On the morning of Sunday, September 3rd, I went across the farmyard to the ancient church. It, with the farm buildings, stood isolated on a small island in the marshes of the one-time estuary of the Parrett River that merged with the Bristol Channel. As I entered I saw, by startling coincidence, engraved in large letters around the font, the word WAR. A few minutes later Wystan joined me to say that we were now at war with Germany.

The grateful dispensation which had arranged our holiday in that remote spot gave us time to get our breath.

(In parentheses, in after years Wystan and I returned to that place. Why had the ancient font those doom-ladened words cut into its Norman stone? The vicar whom we interrogated supposed they must be the initials of the mason who made the font.)

3

In spite of the calamity which had befallen the world, for us personally the years that followed were of exceptional happiness and well-being.

But at first this did not seem possible. My mother bravely insisted on returning home. She could not leave Frank to face what might come alone.

My husband's practice evaporated overnight. Many people evacuated that East Coast area, and the capital which we had put into the firm was lost. We had to begin again. Wystan settled Nicholas and me in South Knighton Farm near my cousins who had come to Bickington in Devon for a while, and he went back to try to salve the wreckage. We said goodbye to one another in the little high-banked Devon lane, and as he drove slowly away I sank to my knees in the road and wept. He went to our friends on the 'Never Mind' and stayed with them while he wound up his office affairs.

To cheer one another we took to writing little articles and comic verses upon any thought that came into our heads, and Simon and Pippa joined in. So that between the lonely farm and the saloon of the 'Never Mind' there was a cheerful shuttle service of our literary scraps. When Nicholas was safely tucked up in bed after supper, I would settle in the solitary parlour, oil lamp on the table, and conjuring up a picture of the cabin of the 'Never Mind', lit by the swinging brass lanterns, with the aroma of coffee permanently steaming on the stove, I would talk on paper to those three, my beloved husband, Simon and Pippa.

Thus we comforted one another somewhat.

Our fortune held throughout. After the somewhat treeless flats of Thanet, Devon seemed a paradise, and I longed to settle here permanently. And it was not many weeks before Wystan was offered the job of Assistant Town Clerk in Exeter. As he was to be in charge of certain Centres in case of air raids, this was a reserved occupation. The Powers that Be had blessed us beyond our merits. We took lodgings in Exeter and began house-hunting.

The house which we called Farthings, of dear memory, was perched high on the hills overlooking Exeter, some two miles out of the city. The prospect was an exaggeration of all that Devon could offer. The ground fell sharply down over hundreds of feet of fields and woods to the River Exe, and in the distance rose the massives of Dartmoor.

It was an eyrie overlooking the most resplendent panorama, a suitable distance from town, shops and school. Soon at night time Wystan was guarding bridges with five rounds of ammunition, or standing on the mounded ancient British camp nearby, behind a single strand of barbed wire, whence he could see over the roof tops of Exeter down the silver estuary of the Exe out to the open sea. Up that waterway the Danes had come to sack Exeter centuries ago. What lay ahead for us?

I had found our little house by what people would call 'luck'. But as ever it seemed to me that a far-sighted visionary was overseeing our affairs. A new acquaintance had taken me to the hill to the north of the city called 'Panorama' to see the view, and from here I spotted the cluster of small houses on the hillside nearby. Of course the position was ideal. So I went from house to house, knocking and asking, 'Is it possible that you wish to let your house?' The third door was the right one. Yes, they did wish to let. (Had they not heard that every house in the West Country had been snapped up by families and evacuees?)

So rejoicing we moved in. Farthings became our home for the next eight years, and in spite of the fluctuating fears and tensions of war, and the most devastating 'blitz' that Exeter had suffered since the coming of the Vikings twelve hundred years before, those were wonderful years for us.

Chapter Five
LIFE SAVING

Some years before, as I said, I had come across Spiritualism. It seemed to me self-evident that survival as described by these intrepid adventurers into the Unknown was plain fact. There was a resonance in me which agreed heart and soul with their discoveries. So much was this the case that I had no interest in psychic investigation, which seemed like laborious experiments designed to prove the obvious. Survival was as true for me as the air we breathe, and I felt I had always known it. My husband shared my views on man's unbroken continuity of life, but we were both sceptical of much that flourishes under the name of fact in this study, and so we never came in contact with a spiritualist association.

However, we were not entirely without experience in this field. When we moved to Devonshire at the beginning of the war, an old friend introduced us to some people who had formed a small group for prayer and spiritual healing, and this group we joined. As a girl I had had some contact with Christian Science, some of my family having been followers of this way of thought, and I had known those who had obtained much benefit from spiritual healing. Belonging to this new group in Devonshire was a woman of singular integrity who was gifted with a certain mediumistic quality. While the group sat in prayer, in full daylight, sometimes it seemed that another entity took her in semi-trance and used her vocal chords to speak. Suddenly she would change, not as to features, but a stronger current of power and voice would suddenly flow through her. We were told that this was her 'Guide'. He gave short lectures upon some spiritual subject.

These experiences were unpretentious and of earnest and reverent character. The half dozen or so people who formed the group were deeply sincere and all were workers for humanity.

The talks given were illuminating but showed no especial originality or high level of intellect and I soon became dissatisfied. I felt that there was so much more needed by way of explanation of the anomalies, the injustices of living which the orthodox religious concepts did not give.

One day, however, something happened that was both evidential and convincing. The circle had sat occasionally in our house and this time six of us were seated quietly in our drawing room. After the address given by the Guide, the medium suddenly turned to me. The Guide's powerful voice continued, 'I have a message for you and a small service for you to do. I want you to communicate at once with A.S. He is about to take his own life. Tell him to do nothing until you have spoken with him. If it can be prevented we must stop that foolish soul from doing something that will set him back upon the path.'

I was startled. A.S. was a man whom my husband and I had known for some years. He had lived abroad during the latter half of his life and had only come to England when war was pending. He now lived some twenty-five miles away and we had visited him when we first came to Devon at the beginning of the war. Our associates in the group did not know of his existence. I knew nothing of his inner thought except that he seemed to be atheistically inclined. His wife had recently died.

When the meeting broke up I sent a telegram to A.S., 'Do nothing until we meet.' He wired back, 'Coming to Exeter tomorrow. Will meet you at Cathedral.'

I went down to the city to wait for him at the West door of the Cathedral wondering what story I should hear. He was there already, pacing up and down in a plainly agitated state of mind. We went into the gardens of the Bishop's Palace and sat down on a seat.

'How did you know?'

'How did I know what?' I countered.

'That I had made up my mind to follow my wife into oblivion?' he said.

Then I told him exactly what had happened and how I had been warned of his decision to take his own life during a prayer circle, by a being from the Beyond.

He was greatly moved. He said that he had decided to do it that very evening and my telegram had reached him just in time.

LIFE SAVING

The consequence of our conversation was far-reaching. Because of my halting dissertation on what I had been gleaning as to what lay beyond death, and the spiritual laws which govern our continued existence, A.S. finally threw over his old nihilistic depression. He began to feel that what he does now is creating his future. He declared himself to be so impressed with the facts of the case that he developed a more hopeful frame of mind. Finally he left his Devonshire home and went to live in Oxford where he enjoyed many years of active and interested life.

My husband and I had now been supplied with a most telling experience.

In my talk with this man, who had the 'logical positivist' kind of intellectualism, I realized that the old spiritualistic way could not carry conviction for this type of mind. Messages given from the Beyond may often be convincing, though many think they may be seen to have some other explanation, issuing from, as Jung would put it, the 'collective unconscious'.

It must be remembered that I am speaking of some thirty years ago. Since then the patient experiments of Professor Rhine in the U.S.A. have at least proved that the human mind has faculties which hitherto have been doubted by the materialistically inclined. Telepathy is now a proven fact, even operating beyond the Laws of Chance in the dull, repetitive laboratory experiments conducted by thousands of students. What Professor Rhine is of course not able to investigate is the result of massive experimentation where the emotions and passions of human beings are involved. In his experiments of the monotonous turning up and guessing of cards, only the lowest frequencies of the human mind can be used, yet even then the faculty of extra-sensory perception has been shown to be fact. Where the human emotions of love, anxiety or fear for the one beloved are used to heat and accelerate the powers of the mind, then the cases of telepathic intunement with a loved one at a distance multiply, as we all know. Such instances are many in the history of mankind, but are impossible of investigation. To attempt to convince the world by telepathic or spiritualist investigation, I felt, could only end in failure. The world turns away from what it does not understand, and it refuses to disturb its old accepted standards in order to broaden its concepts. Tender messages for the bereaved could usually be dismissed as invention or pious wishful-thinking; and so this vital truth, in spite of the patient and convincing work done by the early pioneers of Spiritualism, often renowned men of science, was doomed to be ignored by the intellectual, often, strange to say, because it is 'too good to be true'.

Men fear to trust their optimistic sense of the fitness of things. There is scarcely a human being who does not feel in his heart, 'Of a surety So-and-so lives on.' Yet his rational thought habitually holds him back, and forces a dubious scepticism upon his inner knowing.

It is plain, therefore, that it is an absolute essential that this truth, this knowledge, should take its place, not as a miraculous possibility, a thing which one hardly dare hope for, which needs blind faith to legalize in one's conception of things . . . but as a natural and lawful part of the mechanism of life. Only when the continuity of life could be shown to be the automatic effect of known causes which are eternally in operation – just as a balloon rises if it is filled with gas – only then will the thoughtful, the sceptical, the intellectual, dare to include it in his understanding of life, only then will it become a part of the normal outlook of man and woman, only then will the heart of man be comforted.

The desperate cry of pain of those whose lives have not this truth rang through the curtains of night which enfolded the world in those war years. It was the cry of the human soul as it denies its inner knowing and allows its chill and dense outer thought to face total annihilation for those beloved.

Unthinkable, yet borne by man since life began. Was there no way to spare man this crucifixion . . . this constantly recurring agony?

The *Law* must be discovered and laid bare, not as a pious hope, a resurrecting due to a miraculous overcoming of death, but as a Law, a reaction to cause as automatic as any scientific chain of events, acceptable by all because it is seen to be a part, a very small and natural part, of the Mighty Continuum which we call eternal life.

It was this which spurred on my search.

Chapter Six

PROFIT AND LOSS

I was soon to have intimate experience of this desperate sense of loss.

My brother Rex was posted missing.

He had joined the RNVR at the beginning of the war, putting to use his knowledge of sailing and his Master's Certificate which he had gained when war was threatening. He had been posted to a staff job in Donibristle in Scotland, but this disgusted him, and in letters he would tell of the efforts he was making to get into the thick of things. In early 1940 he got his way, and in charge of a small experimental motor boat he was posted to one of the Channel ports, Folkestone I think. Then, with the evacuation of Dunkirk looming, in his last letter he wrote, 'This is like glorified yachting, only a bit more strenuous. We've just had a spell of duty of ninety hours with no sleep. If anything happens to me look after M. and J.' (his wife and child). And that was the last we heard from him.

We learned later that after four trips across the Channel into the inferno of Dunkirk, retrieving all the men his little boat would take, his MTB had been disabled. Rex had then been given the Frinton lifeboat, and with his crew they had gone back again for another batch. On their return journey a piece of shrapnel had taken him. For gallantry on active service he was mentioned in dispatches.

On receipt of the telegram, 'R. posted missing', from my father, Wystan and I sped to Woking. The trains were stopping everywhere and taking on contingents of our rescued army. Laughing, singing, weary soldiers filled each compartment and spilled over along the corridors. We marvelled at their spirits. They had been grabbed back from hell and could not contain their exuberance. Their boots were sodden and caked with

French sand, their clothes had dried on them. The beaches of Dunkirk were now no more to them than a football scrum.

Roaring with laughter, one said, 'Do you remember old S. wading in with his rifle and pack over his head, until a blooming wave came and swamped him, so he chucked them down into the water and swam for it?'

And another rejoined, 'Yes, and our Sergeant stepped off right into deep water and sunk like a stone with all his stuff hanging about him.'

They hung out of the windows and cottagers gave them cigarettes and cups of tea. Everyone's hearts were overflowing with the colossal relief of the nation to get its army home.

We sat in anguish for my brother, for my parents' anxious waiting. As yet we knew no details. These may be the very men whom Rex had snatched from death—and given his life in the doing.

When the worst was known my father went down to Dover to speak with his men.

'We'd have gone anywhere with him, sir,' said the Second-in-Command. 'There was nothing he did not think of. On our way back in that lifeboat they picked us up with their searchlights, and the blooming brass all over the ship shone like lamps. He made us take off our jackets, anything we could lay hands on, and cover those bits of shining brass. But that was when he copped it. He went down and knew nothing. It was all over at once, sir, and I brought the boat home.'

How was I to comfort my stricken parents? How, how console them?

How could one staunch the wound that thousands were now feeling – of an amputation of one of their family?

Of course I said what I could of my conviction of the continuity of life and personality. I think it did lighten their darkness a little. It was the personal Rex they longed for, not a 'spirit', not an 'angelized soul' unlike the vigorous young man they had known. 'In the arms of Jesus' was not for such as he. When my father wrote to Rex's wife to try to pass on to her a little of the comfort he had taken from our ideas on immortality, she felt they were couched in too religious terms.

'You and I feel nearer to Rex when we talk about him and

laugh together about old times, rather than in the atmosphere of mysticism or seances.'

I saw what she meant. These things were not in Rex's line at all.

The books which I had read on Spiritualism years ago were inclined either to take the tone of darkened rooms and seances, 'spirit rappings' and such like phenomena, or they were of the mystical quality of the 'harmony of the spheres'.

Though both of these angles were approaches to truth, they could not give the solid comfort to wives and parents whose life had been bound up in a beloved and vital personality. Survival of bodily death must be shown to be an automatic and natural law, not a miraculous resurrection. Only this attitude could really reach the heart of the world.

We went back to Devon feeling almost guilty that our home lay in such a peaceful backwater, far from the finalities of war.

Chapter Seven

THE CELESTIAL VISITOR

As I worked at the practice of the Silence my eyes and ears began to open.

During the next summer, answers to my problems began to pour in to my questioning mind. In series of visions, in flashes, in words and sentences. When I came up the stairway into the Silence instruction greeted me. Gradually I began to understand and to formulate a philosophy that made sense out of anomaly, wisdom out of chaos.

I remember one day, it must have been in June or July 1940, for I was lying in hot sunshine in the garden, and the lavender was in full and fragrant bloom. It was afternoon. My son was at school and my husband at his office.

I was thinking deeply, beginning to see a pattern in things which answered some of one's deepest perplexities. But that pattern was so new to me, so startlingly fresh, that I wondered.... Could this be truth that I was mining in the secret places?

Then I heard a voice, 'Go in and take a pad and write.'

I rose and rushed indoors. Taking a writing block I sat down and dashed off a heading: THE WISDOM OF THE SPIRIT.

I wrote a few pages, telling myself that I was starting a new book. 'A perfect understanding of the Laws of Living wipes out all tendency to dis-virtue.'

I worked at hot speed, feeling that I was being impelled to write. Inspiration seemed to pour in.

Then I stopped, dropped the pencil, walked up and down, and finally, calling my dog, I dashed out of the house and across the fields. How could I be certain that what was entering my mind, the visions, the instruction, the answers to my questions – How could I be sure that this was true inspiration? It seemed so desperately important to be sure. My lawyer husband would naturally question these strange ideas. How could he know whether or not I was tapping truth? It was vital for both of us to be certain.

I walked on feverishly, crying out loud within me.

It seemed at that time that my whole life was prayer, and conversation with an unseen, wise and benevolent Being. How urgently I was in need of corroboration of my thought, only the Invisible could know.

Our friends from the 'Never Mind' had by this time moved to London. The yacht had been commandeered by the Military, and they were no longer allowed to live on it. They took lodgings with a friend and Simon continued to paint. He was of an inventive turn of mind and soon he set up a small factory in the country for utilizing certain woods which were plentiful in that district, to help in aircraft production. So we saw no more of them for more than a year – though we kept in touch by letter. Finally, I went down with a nebulous weakness and Pippa came for a short stay to help with the household chores.

She arrived in the middle of November 1941.

I had laid aside the book which I had started, feeling the need for some sort of assurance that the concepts which I was to describe were something more than my own opinions. Instead I pondered a good deal, and filled notebooks with my questings.

One evening, we three were sitting around the fire. I was on the sofa with my legs curled under me and Pippa sat at the other end. It was about eleven o'clock and my husband went off to make some coffee. Pippa said, 'Oh, I feel so sleepy!' Then she slumped over sideways with her head in a most awkward position against my knees.

'Don't go to sleep down here!' I cried. 'Hie thee up to bed!'

Then from Pippa came a few abortive attempts at speech. I looked at her in amazement. Her eyes were closed. Such of the face that I could see from my angle looked unusually remote and serene. Then there came from her slow, carefully chosen words in a voice of an altogether different tone and calibre. This is what was said:

'I am going to try to use this child in this way. There is so much you wish to know, and this is the only way to come to you through a physical instrument.'

At this moment my husband came in bearing cups of hot

coffee. Realizing that Pippa was in a deep trance, I put up my hand sharply and said, 'Sh!'

He stood frozen where he was, listening to the conversation. The lofty voice continued, 'May I suggest that tomorrow evening at about nine o'clock you sit around the fire quietly and I will try to come to you in this way. Do not tell her that this has happened. Do not tell her anything at all. She has a very active subconscious. Even now I am having a little difficulty with it.'

There was a pause.

Startled, I remained silent, wondering whatever I ought to say in this unprecedented situation. I knew that Pippa had never been taken in this way before and that the whole experience was new to her. Then I said that we would do as had been suggested and asked who was speaking to us.

'You will be told later on. It is not necessary now,' was the answer. Then Pippa's throat became husky.

The voice continued, 'This child smokes too much – far too much. Try to get her to smoke less and not at all tomorrow. The throat fills and I find difficulty in using it. I repeat, do not tell her that this has happened. She will not remember anything about it. She will think she has been asleep.'

The voice was measured and illustrious, the accents careful, almost as though used by one who spoke the language rarely. It continued, 'If I were you I would write down the questions that you wish to ask me. But keep it between yourselves as this subconscious is very stubborn. I shall have difficulty with it, but I do not want to have more than I need. I am trying this experiment, I repeat, as it is the only way to come to you through a physical instrument. She will be aware of the forces around her and this may make her a little excited. I will tell you how to banish all alien entities. You say within you, "We are here in the name of Jesus Christ." You will know me by this.' And the arm was raised in a great sign of the Cross. 'This, with very great love and blessing to you all, goodnight.'

The Presence withdrew and Pippa awoke slowly.

'How silly of me, I fell asleep down here,' she said.

My husband and I shooed her up to bed with her cup of coffee. Then Wystan took pencil and paper and wrote down all that we could remember of this astonishing occurrence. Pippa had a Roman Catholic background; she had been educated at a con-

THE CELESTIAL VISITOR

vent and we knew enough about her to know that she had never interested herself in Spiritualism. We had never discussed this type of thing with her, neither had I confessed my inner strivings to her.

When she had retired to bed, my husband and I concocted a list of questions that were uppermost in our minds at that time.

The following evening – it was November 17, 1941 – we sat around the fire once more. Pippa was in an armchair on one side of the fireplace, Wystan on the other, while I had pulled the sofa across the centre between them. My husband had pencil and paper ready. Of course, we had said nothing whatever to Pippa of last evening's happenings, but I had managed to get her not to smoke 'as her throat and chest seemed affected'.

At exactly nine o'clock the wonderful change took place. As a hand is withdrawn from a glove, it seemed as though Pippa was withdrawn from the outer shell of her body while another took her place; or it was like water poured away from a wine glass while a sparkling champagne replenished it.

Then Pippa's form was readjusted to a more upright and dignified posture, the head up, the eyes closed, and a look of serenity spread over her features. A lustre shone from the face that had not been there before and the lips were primed in a look of sweetness. The rich deep tones spoke, 'Good evening. It is nine o'clock!' and the arm was raised giving the sign of the Cross.

We murmured 'Good evening', but were too overawed to say anything further. There was an august air about our celestial Visitor, though we were soon to learn that a vein of humour was often near to the surface. There was in him a calibre of authority which was outside my experience, and a tremendous power emanated from him, redolent of sweetness, love and tolerance.

He waited a few moments and then, leaning forward with a smile, the eyes still fast closed, 'Well, is that all you have to say to me?' His quip broke the ice of our nervousness. He smiled too, and I produced our list of questions.

A sense of peace spread around us, the firelight illumined the room. The standard lamp threw a pool of light over our visitor.

Our first question concerned the relation of the power of thought to healing and prayer. He answered my question patiently and at length. He spoke of the spark of God in each one of us, and the link between that spark and the Divine power. He spoke of love as a healing force. 'I might give you some idea of the power of love,' he said, 'which is the same thing as the power of God, by telling you that everything you see is a manifestation of love. The very atoms of the chair on which you sit, obey the law of love.'

'Then it was you who gave me that thought in precisely those words this morning,' I cried excitedly.

He smiled benignly, nodding his head. 'Excellent, excellent.'

As the conversation continued, I probed further upon the subject of healing in which I had lately become interested. I asked about various techniques. He replied that 'each healer must work out his own technique, each must find his own level'. And then he added, 'And you, my dear child, must not think of trying to heal others until you yourself are healed. Your magnetism is low at present, as is natural if you think a moment. And as to the other aspects of your question, how far one should make oneself a channel, is exactly in like proportion as you are able to be a channel. The greatest Master who ever lived was Jesus Christ. He was the perfect example of the love instrument, he was the perfect channel. Love flowed through him. Love is healing. Healing is love. Love is all good. Love is God. That is, of course, to you almost a platitude. But one cannot say it too often or believe it too strongly.'

'I understand that love comes from the heart. In healing, should one use one's brain in concentrated effort or will the brain get in the way?' (I asked this because I had lately felt a strange force emanating from my forehead like a projectile, which puzzled me.)

'Your brain should be an instrument as the body of Jesus Christ was an instrument. So long, that is, as the brain is not deflecting you from your purpose of healing. If the brain co-operates with this purpose, there is no harm in it: on the contrary, the more you get your purpose into the conscious mind, the more readily it will work for you and those you contact. Concentrate for a few minutes upon a friend who needs healing, then lift your consciousness. You need not think your friend will be forgotten.'

I asked if 'a healer's faith alone is strong enough to create health by the power of his faithful thought, in spite of doubt in the patient's mind'.

'No, unfortunately. It is not impossible that the faith of the one may eventually break down the lack of faith in the other. Where there is lack of faith on the recipient's part, no results can be expected – no lasting and satisfactory result. You cannot force a man to be healed. By prayer and faith it is by no means impossible to take away faithlessness. You must see, however, that while there is lack of faith, the healing power is necessarily blocked.'

'Does that mean that one should teach the spirit before trying to heal the body?'

'No, not necessarily. Some know subjectively. For others faith is not for them in this life. Others acquire faith. To this game there are rules as there are to any other. This is a law. Just as the Law of Gravity does not hold itself up because a little child falls from a top storey window, so, no matter how worthy a man may essentially be, without faith he can achieve nothing. Faith may take many forms. It can be faith in a faith healer, an amulet worn around the neck, or a threepenny piece in the purse! It does not matter through what medium it comes.'

Wystan was scribbling hard all this while trying to get down what was said.

'Then,' I pressed the point, 'Faith is only another word for a tuning in to the God vibration?'

'Exactly. Faith is another word for an opening up, an at-one-ment, a letting in of the divine ray. Oh, the pity of it, for it is so easy! One could laugh and one could weep! There it is waiting for you. You turn against it, making it your own enemy. You must remember,' gently, 'that I do not speak personally.'

I pressed for further information upon the function and working of prayer.

'You are asking me to explain prayer, are you not? Prayer is the desire of the heart expressed. Its technique is roughly this – only roughly – just yet there are factors which you need not know. You make yourself receptive to the divine ray and you ask, and being receptive, you inevitably receive. That is the Law.'

'I understand that for the individual, but how does this work in such a thing as a prayer for peace?' I asked.

'The Law of Merit operates in this too,' was the rejoinder. 'It is necessary for the development of the human race, because of their ignorance and greed which, after all, just means their ignorance.'

And then he turned that lofty visage to me.

'All forms of dis-virtue are ignorance and nothing else. A perfect understanding of the Law wipes out completely all tendency towards dis-virtue. When the prayers of the people become a collective force and faith-full – I say faith-full advisedly – full of faith, and have a real desire for peace, peace will come. This is the Law. You see, you as a unit cannot do much against world karma when things are in their present state. You could have done much at one time, but things are now at a pitch where they must work out their own salvation. When I say you, I mean you as a unit, your husband, your child, all the people you have seen and all the people you have never seen. The power of concentrated prayer is boundless.'

'Then,' I objected, 'it sounds as though it is merely a matter of numbers – how many people pray.'

'While there are people who cannot live in one small house without quarrelling and doing petty things to each other, then you will have wars. While people consider that one piece of land is more God blessed than another, and a nation considers itself more God blessed than another, there will be wars. The sun does not refuse to shine on non-Aryans any more than on Herr Adolf Hitler – bless him! I suppose I have said something that may sound to you very unpatriotic!' And he gave us that glance full of humour.

'No, indeed,' said we.

'There are ways in which that man is great and he might have been a power for good – and will be, in God's good time. He will progress even as you and I.'

Then my husband asked, 'Is it possible to avoid the Law of Cause and Effect by throwing oneself, as people say, upon the mercy of God?'

'No, my dear friend. The Law of Merit, of Action and Reaction must always remain. If I put my hand in the fire and throw myself on the mercy of God, I am a fool! God is Cause and Effect. God is Cause – you are here to learn to develop your souls. While you are in the process of development you are bound to make mistakes through ignorance. God is the perfect parent.

He does not withhold chastisement out of sentimentality. Not that God chastises, men chastise themselves. Are you satisfied with my answer?'

'Yes, thank you very much,' said we.

'Then let us proceed to your next question.' And he leaned back, smoothing the forehead of Pippa with the fingertips murmuring, 'Peace, peace.'

We continued with our list of questions. I asked if, 'When the mind is lifted up into the Silence, or into a wide place of life, is one only benefiting oneself?'

'Oh, my child,' he said, 'do you not know that it is possible for those in a high state of consciousness to sit in an isolated spot and by the power of thought, so to project their thought among men that it has a definite effect upon them? When Jesus Christ was walking among a crowd, all felt better for his passing by, publicans, sinners, scribes, Pharisees, all those who were about at that time.'

I paused and thought for a few minutes, while a wonderful sense of tranquillity hung in the atmosphere.

Then I produced a question which had been puzzling me. 'Does self-hypnotism come into this condition of raised consciousness?'

'Oh yes,' he answered. 'It is a form of self-hypnosis – or rather de-hypnosis. From the womb on, you are in a dream state. In the case of the elevation of the consciousness to the Ego, the Spirit, you are coming out of unreality into reality. As I stand here I am by no means open to all the Rays, but what I see is with such perfection as I have achieved or attained. To whatever plane one finds onself attuned, that may be considered the limit of the present capacity. It is not, of course, a permanent limit. One can be raised by prayer and development along the lines Christ has shown you. Is that quite clear to you? If not, tell me now.'

'Yes,' said I, gratitude welling in me. And I strove to express my gratitude for the miracle of his coming.

With a grace which we came to associate with this Visitor from another world, he answered, 'I beg that you do not thank me, but the Most High. You must realize that I do but obey instructions and do my duty.'

Then my husband asked a question. 'Surely the senses of the body are of value?'

'Oh yes, indeed,' he replied. 'Very much so. But your body prevents you from seeing beyond the Wall of Maya.'

'The Wall of Maya?'

'The Wall of Maya . . . your illusion. You will come across the expression in Eastern philosophy. The body is like an optical illusion. You have the illusion of parallel lines meeting on the horizon. From where I stand I see things differently.'

Here Wystan asked some unrecorded question about the next plane of living, to which the answer was given, 'You will learn in time that quite a different set of values is required to appreciate and understand the essentials of a vibration not your own. You must try not to lose sight of the fact that people do not alter merely because they lose their bodies.'

Sometimes the recorded conversation was a little disjointed, because Wystan, who was taking down as fast as he could, had lost the thread. I asked, 'Will you tell us who you are? Are you a guide?'

'I am your Friend in God,' he answered. And added: 'I am not attached, not a Guide.'

Suddenly I felt giddy and faint. He, without my having made any sign at all, said sharply, 'Put your head right back! You must be careful of your heart for a little while. Not too much movement for a few weeks.' Then he gave some detailed instruction as to diet.

We had come to the end of our hastily improvised questionnaire. I said, 'Oh, there is so much I long to ask you, but I can't think quickly enough!'

'There is no hurry. There is all eternity in which to ask and to receive,' was his reply.

I asked if he would come again to speak with us. He said that he would come the following night 'if conditions were suitable'. He explained that so much depends upon 'atmospheric conditions and our vibrations which were by no means always the same'.

'How can we improve them?' asked Wystan.

'Through thought,' was the reply.

'What sort of thought?' Wystan persisted.

Our Visitor looked at him amusedly.

'My dear Wystan, why will you be so obtuse? Pray forgive the familiarity.'

We enjoyed the sparkle of fun that scintillated in the air. I then made some remark about someone we knew who had recently died, who, I said, 'was on a lower plane'.

'On a lower plane?' He leaned forward with a quizzical look.

'Well, I . . . I . . . imagine that you. . . .' I stammered.

'Ah,' he said smiling, 'I see that you are fishing as to whether I am a Brass Hat or Red Tab!'

'Oh, no, no!'

'You may fish but the waters are deep. Mind your own business, bless you!' And he leaned back with a look of secret amusement.

Here the conversation turned to Pippa and Simon.

'Shall we tell Pippa about this now?' I asked.

'Yes, you may tell her now.'

Wystan then asked for a definition of genius.

'A genius is a man who is open to inspiration,' was the reply.

'Men of science,' said Wystan, 'say that genius is a matter of physical make-up.'

'There is mighty talk of genes in the make-up of a man, and it is said that these and these alone are responsible for his character. To a certain extent this is indeed so, but it is rarely, if ever, considered that the placement of certain genes in the body is effect and not cause.'

There was a pause while Wystan strove to get it all down on paper.

Then our Mentor asked if we had any more questions to pose.

'I am interested,' said Wystan, 'in the condition in the life immediately beyond this one. For instance, how R. lives, and what are his surroundings.'

'You must remember again my analogy of trying to put a gallon of milk into a pint pot. R's realization of his new surroundings is limited by his imagination, which, as you know, was never very strong. He is not so very different from the young man who died a little over a year ago . . . I use the word "died" as being the least affected!'

'But surely,' objected Wystan, 'it must seem strange to him that he does not meet any of his friends?'

'Now don't tell me that if you were suddenly transported to another level of existence you would be worried that you did not meet any of your friends! Everyone finds himself in those surroundings akin to his development. The understanding of those who pass over is often confused by the lack of previous accurate instruction on the subject.'

'Can you tell me if there is pain in his world?' asked Wystan.

'To some extent, yes. If I were to pinch him he would certainly yell, and most likely try to punch me on the nose! But,' very softly, 'I should not feel it.'

Then after a pause he said, 'I have to fight against Pippa's subconscious.'

Wystan asked, 'May we take it that Pippa's thoughts have not influenced your words?'

'Yes, I have been successful as I have been working on her most of the day.'

'We do thank you most profoundly,' I said, 'for all the care you have taken.' I did not know how to express my gratitude.

'I am not what is called a "guide". I am of a Body which is called upon on occasion to give out little teachings as they become necessary.'

Pause. I had an idea.

'You know in this world people are always asking for tests. Would you care to provide us with a test?'

'Do not try tests. They will always find a way to explain it. They will say that it is telepathy, or the subconscious, or,' with humorous emphasis, ' "world memory"! A beautiful phrase that, it gets away with almost everything! Never try tests, it is to be discouraged. I want you in general in future, however, to regard with suspicion everything that comes through in this way.'

'With suspicion?'

'With suspicion,' he said firmly, but refused to be drawn further except to add, 'Always use your own shrewd intelligence in such matters.'

He paused, and then continued, 'This is a stubborn child! I think if I were to use her until the end of her life I should not get any voice through but her own or any gesture that is not hers.'

I asked a question as to the nature of power in a personality.

'Power,' he responded, 'is the radiation of the ego transmitted through the instrument of the body into a magnetic emanation sometimes called the aura. Now I will release this child.'

'Will you come to us tomorrow night?' I hardly dared ask.

'Yes. If it is possible. I would advise a little earlier. You should have been in bed an hour ago, but,' smiling, 'it will not do you much harm!'

'And may Pippa smoke tomorrow?'

'Yes, I think she may have one cigarette after each meal. And now goodnight and God bless you all.'

The sign of the Cross was given. The Presence withdrew. Smoothly, as a glass empties, the celestial wine vanished. Pippa's form seemed to relax and shrink, the illustrious expression melted away. She opened her eyes slowly and looked at the clock on the mantelpiece, which stood at eleven o'clock.

'Good heaven!' she exclaimed. 'I've ruined the evening by going to sleep! Why ever didn't you wake me!'

Her humdrum grin was hard to bear after the grace we had lately known.

And then we told her about these strange happenings.

It was difficult for her to feel the truth of what we told her, since she never was able to enjoy the full flavour of the puissant presence who entered our room to converse with us. To her it was as if we were telling her of a dream of which she had no recollection whatever; it seemed as if she had just awoken from a dreamless and refreshing sleep.

2

The following evening we sat again around the fire. Earlier, and unknown to Pippa, my husband and I had struggled with his notes. Much was scrappy and illegible and we found it hard to fill in the conversation as it had really occurred.

This time we were prepared and waiting for the celestial Visitor a good deal earlier.

After a few moments, Pippa's appearance changed as before. She faded out and a greater personality seemed to expand her form. It is curious, on reflection, how this impression of size became implicit in these interviews. Pippa is of medium stature, a good deal shorter than I, yet when her soul had been withdrawn from her body, and supplanted by one of the calibre of our celestial Visitor, my husband and I felt ourselves in the presence of largeness and of radiant Power. It is true that the form was used differently; instead of the slack appearance of a woman resting in the armchair, suddenly there was the upright yet relaxed poise, the head held high on the shoulders, a sense of regal dominance transfigured the form, the face became of a noble dignity, emanating serenity, tolerance and love.

When, as happened gradually, my eyes began to open, and I saw the features which were sometimes superimposed over the lineaments of Pippa, I realized why her face became so altered. It was as if a five-watt bulb had been replaced by a hundred-watt lamp. In later times he referred to 'the mask I am able to make over the face of Pippa' (rendered in etheric energy). When Pippa was returned to us after these interviews, I used to need to turn away to recover somewhat, for watching her once more, as it were, 'engage' in the mechanism of her own features, was a shock which took Wystan and me a while to get used to.

This evening, after a few minutes, the eyes closed and the wonderful transformation took place. The arm described the great sign of the Cross. The rich and authoritative tones spoke. 'Good evening. I think I am a little early; but you are in trouble with your notes, are you not? May I suggest that we look through them. I say this because of what is to come.'

Gratefully we read through the notes and while our Mentor patiently dictated the amendments, Wystan wrote them in.

'I think what we said was. . . .' he would say, and Wystan added the corrections, though in fact much was omitted from the two-hour discourse. When we had completed the task, our Mentor continued, 'Now about this child. You were right when you told her to rest. I did not even have to impel you to say it. In that connection I can impel you to think or say things, but never compel; you make your own choice. Free will is never interfered with.'

And he added some details about Pippa's health. Then he went on, 'Now Clarice, my child. About the little matter of the ivory amulet.' Pippa and I had been arguing a point earlier with regard to a small ivory figurine which had been given me.

'I want you to know that it is the attitude of mind that counts in a case like that, and not the things in themselves. Your attitude was the right one.'

'Thank you,' said I. Then, perplexed by the closed eyes which turned towards me smilingly, 'May I ask if you can see us?'

'Of course I can see you!' But he would not elaborate. Wystan

THE CELESTIAL VISITOR

now said, 'I should like to raise a question on the subject of faith. It seems to me that there is a vast difference between a person's faith in an amulet and his faith in God.'

'Yes, there is a vast difference,' was the reply, 'but it is one of degree only.'

Wystan evidently still looked puzzled.

'Are you satisfied with my answer?'

'Yes, I think I am,' said Wystan.

'Do you think you are satisfied, or are you really satisfied?' he said quizzically.

Wystan still felt perplexed and made some unrecorded query.

'Now, Wystan, there is a question behind that question. Let us have it!'

'There still seems to me,' Wystan struggled to express his perplexity, 'to be a fundamental difference between the faith of a man on a ship, who thinks a lucky charm will keep him from harm and the man who has faith in God.'

'I see exactly what you mean. A soul or ego who is at a certain stage of development, but who has the gift of faith (which must be earned), often puts his faith in – or uses as a channel for his faith – some little idol having no intrinsic significance, but yet which proves a viaduct for faith. In the case of a highly developed ego there is no need for outward and visible media. The ultimate result is the same. It is the working of the same law by different machinery. Do you understand what I mean? In each case the power of God flows in. It is the degree which is different.'

'Yes, I see now what you mean,' answered Wystan.

'Pippa wished me to ask if we might have a name to think of you by?' I asked.

'Does it matter?'

'Well, a little!'

'You must see that we all have had many names. Now don't tell me that you are a master of diplomacy and are fishing again?'

The atmosphere was warm and we laughed.

Pippa's throat became husky.

'She has been smoking too much again,' he said.

'I expect she forgot,' I excused her.

'She did not forget one cigarette! But we must not expect too much from her!'

79

I said, 'In this world scientists seem to impute so much that is inexplicable in man to the subconscious. Could you explain the subconscious to us?'

'I think I can give you a working idea of those various strata of mind possessed by man. There is not only the subconscious mind, as so many scientists presuppose, bless them! How presumptuous are the scientists! But there are in reality minds vibrating into infinity . . . mind within mind within mind. Each is especially suitable in its essence to the varying planes upon which it will eventually function, rather, you know, like a nest of Chinese boxes, or a nest of wooden eggs, one within the other.'

'Then,' said I, 'the mind of man is like a universe in itself.'

'Exactly, and his body is a universe too. The subconscious is the so-called "astral" mind. When men die they shed a skin. Like the skin of a snake, each is just sloughed off as it ceases to be needed.'

'Scientists tell us also that our actions are governed almost entirely by instincts. For instance, is it true that some fears are derived from our ancient jungle life?'

'To some extent they are right. What the scientists are apt to confuse is potentiality with actuality. Instinct in a highly evolved man is more or less potential – and less actual. His conscious control increases. The subconscious mind is an actuality.'

I had stoked up a large fire before starting the evening's session, and this was now glowing hotly. A little earlier I had risen and put a cushion between the fire and Pippa's leg, fearful that the heat would be uncomfortably great.

Suddenly our Mentor turned to me and said, 'What is worrying you, Clarice?'

'I am afraid that that cushion will scorch!' said I.

With a rising crescendo of amusement he said, 'When the leg becomes too hot I will remove it further away from the fire, bless you!'

Then he added, 'I want you to understand that when two vibrations are in harmony one with another no misunderstanding is possible. Mark what I say.' And he repeated the sentence again, while I wondered why he had given out this statement with so much emphasis, but later on it was to become clear.

He continued in jesting fashion, 'You were discussing earlier, before I spoke to you tonight, the problem of the "little animals". How did you put it? I seem to remember a pretty little rhyme. . . ?'

'Do you mean about the "little animals eaten by the cannibals"?' (I had been quoting a comic song and suggested that men were cannibals to eat animals.)

Leaning back in his chair with a dry smile, he murmured softly, 'That was it . . . the "little animals eaten by the cannibals!" I will give you this as a heading. Animals, when they leave your world, join a form of group-consciousness. I will not say more than this tonight. You will notice that I do not tell you very much through this instrument. It is merely my duty to drop certain seeds into your mind. Will you think about it, please.'

'I long to deepen my knowledge,' I said. 'I feel it is so shallow – like thin ice upon a pond.'

He smiled and nodded his head approvingly. 'Excellent, excellent! Your knowledge will deepen all in good time.'

'But I am impatient!'

'I like your impatience, Clarice. Such impatience is divine, only it must be channelized. Your search for wisdom is divine. I will help you. If you use them thoughtfully, the little seeds which I drop into your mind will fructify. You are just at a stage when you need a little assistance, to make sure that you are on the right path. But after a time you will be able to answer all these questions within yourself.'

'But I do not want to lose my Teacher.'

'You will never lose your teacher – your helper, Clarice.'

I was silent, struggling to realize the portent of this. Then I asked, 'Will you tell us the relationship of our subconscious to sleep?'

'The purpose of sleep is to keep a man in contact with his ego, his spirit, his other Self. No man must be allowed altogether to forget that he is something more than a collection of chemicals. Sleep is a renunciation, a living for a while in connection with the Spirit of all things. We will spend an evening on this question another time. I will then go into the effects of taking a narcotic, a blow on the head, and so on.'

'You know I have been reading. . . .' I began.

'You know? Do not grant me omniscience!'

'Er – well. . . .' I stammered, but I was sure all the same that he *did* know! And I explained that I had been reading of the theory that we all meet in sleep if we wish. I was fishing again.

'I should say that that is a little far-fetched. But there is a continual process of filtration from the astral or subconscious mind into the conscious and back again. That explains many things – for example, in some of the most unexpected people you will find things of the Spirit because of the filtration which is going on.'

'When our minds are functioning in the astral, is it individuals in the astral who influence us or is it. . . ?' (I had half formed in my mind to say, 'Is it our own conscious minds gaining knowledge there?' but stopped, groping for words).

'Yes?' he said, leaning forward. 'Yes?'

After thinking for a moment or two, I said, 'Oh, I see! It is the same thing!'

He leaned back, again saying, 'Excellent, excellent! I wanted you to see that.'

Then I said, 'I have heard the suggestion that after a certain stage one becomes part of a group consciousness. Does one then retain one's individuality?'

'Yes. Into the fifth plane individuality, almost as we know it, remains. Beyond, I am not in a position to speak.'

Here Wystan asked some questions upon the subject of evolution and about the sabre-toothed tiger which, as he said, 'seemed to rule the earth for so long and then died out. It seems as though God made a mistake in His experimenting'.

'God does not make mistakes! I want you to get away from the idea of the separateness of life. All life is one – not lots of separate lives, turning into "dead ends", but one life behind all, using first this and then that form – it is the God-stream of life. The soul starts in Infinity – passes through the stages of development, and goes on to Infinity. Life is inextinguishable.'

'Then it is life seeking to find a perfect expression?' said I.

'Yes. The so-called "dead-ends" occur because atmospheric and other conditions change, and that particular line of life is no longer suitable.'

'If animals join a group consciousness at death, do they join a sort of field of Spirit, and then come back finally as a man?' I asked.

'The ape who has earned for himself perception and self-awareness goes back at death into the world of Spirit, and comes back next time as a man.'

'But animals and men seem so different.'

'The difference is not so great as you imagine. They both have two arms, two legs and a head. Furthermore, it takes very much longer than a single lifetime on earth for a soul to develop itself into the capabilities of a philosopher, a musician or a sage. Men live many lives on earth with sometimes long periods of rest and holiday in the world of Spirit, before they expand their content, their capacity, sufficiently to gain their "wings of no return". It is sometimes possible, at a certain stage of development, to achieve memory or vision of parts one has played in past centuries. These might be called "flashbacks".'

'And do we meet again on Earth those whom we have loved in past lives?'

'Yes. Where you see more than a little of a person then you have met before. Often it is an old link.'

'And do we in our lives keep the same features?'

'Yes, but with small differences. The reason is that we construct ourselves through our own habit of thought.'

'How much do we inherit from our parents?' This was a question that bothered me.

'Nothing except physical things. Those on Earth are born to the parents whom they either merit or deserve. You must remember my saying that the genes in the body are result and not cause. Your own genes – or their counterparts in spirit – exert magnetic action upon the type of parentage.'

Then a sudden thought struck me. 'Surely all that you are teaching us is not for us alone. Should it not be put down in a book and published?'

I thought now that I knew for certain the source of my inspiration at the start of my book *The Wisdom of the Spirit*.

Said he with whimsical emphasis, 'That is *my* idea. You have reached a stage of development when your thought would interest others, and I thank God there are many.'

'And should the book come confessedly from you?'

'It is too early to decide that.'

'But how, since Pippa is going home tomorrow, shall I keep in touch with you?'

I felt I knew the answer, but I had to ask.

'You go into the Silence once or twice a day. In the Silence you will find truth. I have only used this expedient to come to you because a little help was necessary. Soon this method will be necessary no longer. You will notice that while upon "ground level", as it were, we can only speak of "ground level" things.'

My mind was racing like a steam engine which sometimes skids when it starts out of a station. There were a thousand things that I wanted to ask, but it seemed that I could not put them into words.

Wystan, who had been writing hard all this time, getting down as much as he could of the conversation without a knowledge of shorthand, so that inevitably a good deal is omitted, here asked a question about Time.

'That is a tremendous question. It is too late to go into it now. All I will say tonight is that you who live in the dimension of Time cannot possibly understand timelessness.'

'But surely,' Wystan persisted, 'in the next plane one can speak of one event happening before or after another?'

'Yes, certainly Time persists in the next few planes, but not quite in the same form as you know it.'

'Oh,' I cried naively, 'I should like to get to the bottom of that!'

He gave a dry smile and spoke under his breath, 'I too should like to get to the bottom of that!'

Then I spoke of the group I had lately formed for spiritual study.

'Which is an excellent thing,' he broke in. 'My child, you are perfectly competent to speak to them yourself.'

'But how can one be sure not to put a block across what inspiration one has by one's own insufficiency? It seems so important.' This, to me, was the crux of the matter.

'Who said it would be inspirational speaking? Tell them what you know. I rarely prophesy, but in this case I will make a prophecy: Once you have spoken the first word the rest will be easy; and I shall be so glad, so glad. And now I must release this child. We will have further discussion another time.'

I was anxious, unwilling to let the situation slip away.

'But Pippa is leaving tomorrow,' I said again.

'I know. But I intend to try to use her hand for automatic writing in case it may prove helpful. It will be difficult and may take months. But remember what I told you. You are not alone in your quest.'

'Shall we tell Pippa to practise?'

'No, no! She needs very different treatment. She is a difficult horse to ride! She should never consider herself a trance medium. She can be used in this way, but she would never be excellent.'

Here Wystan made a remark which elicited the reply, 'I think we must trust to the plan of God, though I am sure the plan of Wystan would be a very good one!'

And then he said more seriously, 'In case you should try to get in touch with me when I am not available, remember what I have told you as to how to banish all undesirable influences: a little prayer within the mind, and the words: "We are here in the name of Jesus Christ!"'

I was full of gratitude, for on each occasion our celestial Visitor had been with us for over two hours.

'We do thank you so gratefully for coming to us.'

And he replied with gentleness, 'Thank you for having me! And now goodnight and bless you, my dear friends in God.'

It was sixteen years before that 'first word' was spoken.

Chapter Eight

FURTHER INTERVIEWS

1

After that, of course, I redoubled my efforts to extend the capacity of the mind in the Silence, and gradually the teaching poured through. I had received the corroboration which I so urgently wished for. I knew now that what was coming into my mind was not fancy, wishful thinking, neurosis, or a product of the 'collective unconscious'. I knew at last that – as our Teacher had said – I was 'not alone upon the quest'. Whereas before I had had faith in the sense of guidance and companionship of the Powers of Spirit, now it was proven for my lawyer husband as well as myself. The subtle and audacious 'parachute landing' which had come unsolicited into our very drawing room, had taken our breath away, but the impact of an illustrious being totally different from the personality of Pippa, had been more than convincing. Furthermore, as time went on, in the interviews that followed, our other-worldly Visitor continued to show knowledge of events before they happened and frequently gave evidence of being able not only to read my mind, but to be entirely informed as to the thought processes that I had used. I had found the source of the instruction which was filling my mind during the times of concentration and the flashes of vision which had come to me all my life. Not only had the source declared itself outwardly, but often the same words were used, and always, of course, aspects of the same – to me – new philosophy, which struck me with the impact of a new revelation.

As our Visitant had made it clear, it was plainly his policy to discourse as little as possible upon the metaphysical problems with which my mind was struggling. His purpose was only to reassure me, to let me know that I 'was on the right path'. The 'seed thoughts' which he threw out were sufficient not only to clear my mind of doubts as to their source, but it proved this for my husband's benefit as well.

With regard to the book which I had started to write, I realized that it was an impossibility to see the cosmic landscape as a whole with sufficient clarity to describe in words the scaffolding, the stresses and strains of the universal order, as I was beginning to glimpse it. Indeed, there were no words available descriptive of these powers. But it had been made clear to me that I must attempt it, and I knew now that a sure hand was guiding me in the attempt.

Many small signs showed this. In my experimenting amongst the levels of mind within, in the early stages I used all sorts of expedients to aid concentration. On bright days, when sunshine streamed in through the windows and sounds in the lane outside multiplied, I experimented with a scarf bound round my eyes to try to exclude the outer world. This was permitted for a while, and I found it did help up to a point, but soon a clear vision was held in front of my inner eye showing myself with two black patches glued over my eyes. So this must be discarded as likely to prove restricting.

I used to complain to myself that I had never found any books upon meditation, nor had been led to study the ancient philosophies or eastern religions. To curb this complaint a vision of a baby's bottle was held in front of my inner seeing, and the words were spoken into my mind: 'It is easier to fill an empty vessel.'

So, as I practised, with confidence enhanced by those three wonderful evenings, and by the sureness of this inner guidance, my mind became more focused. I used the ardency of heart and concentration of will in striving to lift the conning-tower hatch which normally seals the skylight of the mind. Sometimes I strove, struggled and slid backwards. Often in disappointment and despair I chid myself for making no progress. But as I look back now, progress was really being made.

I took up again my old habit of diary writing, and found it eased me greatly. It became a release and a stabilizer, and as I recorded the steps of the inner way, it became a meditation in itself. I had so often felt the sort of thirst for the light that a plant must feel that knows inwardly its need for the benizen of sunlight, even while a stone is laid over its head. And just as a plant, by its effort, can thrust aside the stone or burst through concrete or macadam and force its way out into the sunshine, I found that the mind of man can do this also.

Now, out of the planes of the Hereafter, a hand was held towards me; not from a Being remote and mystical, but from one who had once been human. Someone who had conquered now leaned down towards me, taught me, and held out a hand to steady my climb. In order to do this, he had clothed his Spirit's form in tangible human attire for a few hours, and had spoken through physical vocal chords which made so comforting an impact upon my physical ears. He had used such expressions as, 'From where I stand things look different', and 'He will progress even as you and I'.

Above all, that which had been apprehended with the inner faculties had now been endorsed by outward happenings. The corroboration which I so earnestly sought had been given. I felt elated and worked harder at my efforts to climb the slippery stairway.

The Holy Fire was still the goal, the lamp and the oil, but now, so seemingly close to me in the invisible, was a master-hand to guide me. I realized that this was he who had guardianed me throughout my life, of whom I had so often been conscious, whose words and teaching I had received and who had engineered so very many blessings for me. The exhilaration of this discovery made me vault over the mountain peaks of thought till I landed upon a plane where it was possible to receive the teaching direct.

This did not happen at once, of course. I was weak in health still, and so permitted to spend a good deal of time idly resting, apparently doing nothing. But in truth I was working hard, assaying the climb aloft.

By the Christmas of that year I seemed to be making progress, but by no means fast enough for my liking.

Our two friends were with us for the holiday, and during that period two sessions were allowed us with our celestial Visitor. I will give a digest of what was said.

On the first occasion he was suddenly with us, without warning or expectation. The two men were out. Suddenly Pippa was withdrawn and he was there. As time went on I became accustomed to this smooth and masterly transition, and we learned to accept his appearance as one does a sudden burst of sunshine, but not to make demands.

After the sign of the Cross he greeted me, 'Good evening, my dear child. Were there not some especial questions which you wanted threshed out, as you say, in the open air?'

'Yes, indeed,' I cried, 'but I can't remember a single one without my notebook!'

'Why not fetch it then?' he said amused.

I fled upstairs for my notebook. Settled once more by the fire, I said, 'I am anxious to tear down the veil between this world and the next. It seems that so much suffering could be saved....'

'The veil will not be torn down. It will melt.'

'But I want to help people to understand. It would give so much comfort.'

And he spoke then at some length as to how we cannot learn people's lessons for them. Each one must climb his own ladder of experience – for some it takes many lives. 'Conditions in this world will never be perfect – it would lose its value as a training ground. You must not think, however, that I am preaching a doctrine of depression.'

'But surely one can help people?' I said.

'Certainly one can help people. Those who have brought themselves to the brink of knowing may be helped enormously. The books which you write will do this. Such books rarely get into the hands of those to whom they might do harm. Life is a progression, a gradual expansation of consciousness and of faculties gained from the divine powers through experience. The path you are engaged upon is difficult and dangerous, it is necessary to exercise wisdom, balance and common sense. You must keep your feet upon the ground. The purpose of all spiritual practices is to teach self control, discrimination and judgement. Without these we flounder. Man has to learn that when he gives up the desire and the struggle for happiness through the senses, and learns to look within himself, only then does he find peace and inner joy. I think you know this well enough.'

I asked a question about memory.

'Memories,' he answered, 'are passed through the subconscious or astral mind and negatived there. Imagination is the product of the objective passed through to the subjective. You will understand more of this later on.'

'You once said, "When one raises one's consciousness to one's ego." Is one's ego then God?'

'Yes, one's ego is indeed God.'

'Can one then add to God?'

'Yes, it sounds ridiculous, doesn't it. But God is being added to all the time. Think of cellular life. Think a moment. Do not talk – just think.'

I thought. I thought of cellular life. I thought of evolution and how the single cell is built up into more complex structures. . . .

'That is right,' he said, watching me.

I thought of the gradual mounting up of the sum total of life on this planet, from amoeba to man. Yes, I could see that God is being added to all the time. I seemed to gain thought-pictures and understanding from my proximity with him. Then he said, 'But for the sake of your humility I want you to realize that it is impossible for you to understand fully the nature of God. For the sake of your humility I say this.'

I burst out with, 'Oh, I wish I could see you! I am impatient of my limited vision.'

He leaned forward and spoke with emphasis. 'I will tell you this: that you have neither seen nor heard – mark what I say – you have neither seen nor heard the last of me yet.'

I, in an endeavour to understand what was behind his words, repeated them slowly, and then said, 'What is the meaning behind those words?' For I was beginning to learn that much that he said in this fashion carried a double meaning.

'Just a seed!' he said.

After consulting my notebook again I asked if the 'process of reincarnation goes on and on?'

He was enigmatical as I was to find so often was his way. The seeds were what I must think over.

'You remember what I told you of the minds of man – mind within mind within mind.'

'Is that an answer?' I asked.

'It is just another seed!' he smiled.

'And do you remember all your lives on earth?' I asked.

'Yes, I have reached that stage of development,' he answered quietly.

There was a pause. I loved those little pauses. They gave me time to realize the unrealizable.

Then I asked a technical question which demanded a complicated answer.

'That is a question which I do not propose to go into just now,' he said, and I understood that because of my weakness he did not wish me to think deeply. True, my head did swim when I thought to any extent, but I wanted so much to draw him out upon so many problems.

Then he spoke again. 'This is the last time I will speak with you for a while. Your health is such that I want you to think of practically nothing else but getting well. I want to see you with a much stronger physical vibration around you. I want to see you returned to the full splendour of your health.'

I was silent. I knew now that speech was scarcely necessary, that he knew what I was thinking. Then he said, 'Do you remember the story of Icarus?'

'No,' I said blankly.

'Icarus' father made him a pair of wings because he wanted to fly to the sun. But the wings were of wax. Icarus flew too near to the sun and his wings melted, and he fell into the Aegean Sea and was drowned.'

I sat in silence wondering what this had to do with me.

He looked at me with a twinkle.

'It is a Greek myth, in which, as in most myths, there is contained a truth.'

There was a pause.

'I want you to keep your feet square upon earth until you are strong again.'

I did not want my feet square upon earth. Already he had given me enough to give them wings. But now he was going to withdraw. I railed at my physical weakness.

'And now, Clarice, I must leave you.'

'And if I send you a strong thought does it reach you?'

'That depends upon the vibration upon which you send it, and upon the vibration I am contacting at the time. But you will not be left without certain little aids.'

Then he spoke vigorously. 'And now, my blessed Clarice, think only of getting strong. Remember this is a separation only in appearance. It will be no more of a separation than it was during these last six weeks. Only in this way I shall not speak with you. I want to see you quite strong before I cram you with knowledge.'

My heart leapt at the anticipation.

'Cram me with knowledge! What a delectable thought!' I exclaimed.

He smiled.

'Never cease your divine search for wisdom,' he said, 'and always remember that I love you, that I may be with you even though you cannot see me, that it will not be for very long. And now goodnight, and God bless you, my child.'

With the sign of the Cross he withdrew.

2

Now I quote from my journal, March 8, 1942:

'After many weeks of despair, intense elation and delight, after struggle with the weakness of my body, after discoveries and experiences in other dimensions, after misgivings and many wrestlings, I craved the comfort of cool words heard with the ears, even if they did contain chidings. I tried to think about nothing but getting stronger, but it was no use. I was caught as if by a magnet and drawn towards the delectable planes above. I could not give that up. And so, needless to say, I continued my upward striving.'

My husband and I had arranged to spend Easter with Pippa and her husband, and so at their house, after an interval of three months or more, an interview with our Teacher was granted.

We had learned by this time that he rarely gave dissertations. Unless we questioned him he would sit silent. I had found that one can only learn from a Teacher what the pupil is able to draw from him. One had to mine the diamonds which lay within that august exterior, and even then one would possibly be put off with an oblique response that it might take weeks to understand. Nothing was given free.

On this occasion, at my commenting upon this, he said, 'My dear child, I could easily carry you up the stairs, but if I did so you would soon lose the use of a very good pair of legs!'

Then I burst out with, 'I feel that I have lived a thousand lives since Christmas. What have I been doing?'

Gently he answered, 'You have been trying to live the Hereafter now; and you have been experiencing visions.'

'And the mountain?' I referred here to certain experiences

which had overtaken me in an expanded state of consciousness, which I will describe presently.

'Was a vision,' he answered. 'Experiences such as these are sometimes a corollary to a state of mind arrived at.'

'How can I know that I am not merely wishful thinking?'

'There is wishful thinking, as our cheerful propagandists term it, and there is constructive wishful thinking.'

'Oh!' Light broke into my mind for a moment.

'Have you found something?' he queried.

'Yes!' I suddenly saw the link, the creative aspect, between constructive wishful thinking or visualization, and prayer, which is the 'desire of the heart expressed'.

'Excellent, excellent,' he murmured, watching me.

'Is that what I have been doing all my life?' said I, referring to the bounties that had showered so often upon me, giving me the reputation among my friends of being 'lucky'.

'That, together with the reaping of certain fruits earned.'

I fell silent, thinking. Then, 'Won't you explain, tell me what I am doing? Won't you prescribe? Must I always grope in the dark?' I wished so much that he would give me verbal instruction on the technique of meditation.

'It is always necessary to grope in the dark until you work out your own technique for yourself,' he said.

'But these feelings in my head, my forehead, my eyes. . . ?'

'It is the quickening of the seed,' he said.

'Shall I be able to see better presently?'

'To see is upon the Path of Wisdom. Explanations of the physical reactions only tend to confuse.'

Here I forget how the conversation ran. More and more we tended to converse obliquely, as it were, each knowing the other's mind, so that only the fewest words were needed as outward symbols of our train of thought.

A sentence stuck in my memory, and is in the recorded notes:

'It is interesting to study collective reactions. I will speak to you on this sometime. Collective reactions creating vibrations which in turn create conditions – and so on.'

He was referring to events in Germany at that time.

'How can I know what is true in my consciousness?' I asked him later. 'So as not to dupe myself?' This was obviously all important – though I had learned that my Mentor would find a way to keep me straight.

'I have already told you this. You go into the Silence. There you will find truth. I want you to believe and know that I am with you, helping you.'

I did not know how to express my gratitude. Stumblingly I spoke of this.

'No,' he said. Then, 'I want you to understand that every word I say to you, however small, has a specific meaning.'

Then I asked him a question which sounded to me inquisitive, so I caught it back with the words, 'Forgive me'.

He answered, 'All forgiveness between you and me was wiped out thousands of years ago.'

Suddenly his voice rang out with startling force.

'Give me your hands.' I put my hands in his. He held them by the tips, and conveyed them in a strange gesture up to within about a foot of 'his' face. I knew that he caught them thus so that they could imbibe an invisible emanation of power from his being. He held them thus while he spoke, 'I will be your helper'. He spoke of the road all must travel. 'You have to decide whether to go to the left or to the right, or to keep straight on.' And then his brows, usually so serene, became deeply troubled, and he seemed to be filled with a great compassion. 'The Path of Wisdom contains exaltation, delight, rocks, dangers and precipices – and realization. I will help you. But the time is rapidly coming when I shall be able to help you less and less, and you will be able to help yourself more and more; and you will think you are able to help yourself not at all, but that is inevitable.'

The power of his vibration was like a cloak about me, a shield of strength. I could say nothing for a few moments. I was struggling to realize the unrealizable. Then I said, 'I want to be able to help the world.'

'You underrate the resources of power upon which you can draw,' he answered.

A little later I recalled that an intimate friend and member of our group had asked me to ask him a question about her life.

'In fact,' said he crisply, 'she wishes me to tell her fortune for her. I absolutely refuse to tell her fortune! Tell her to do the work she is doing with the best heart possible, and ways will be found, paths will open.'

I asked if those who felt a tie in this life had met in previous lives.

'As I told you earlier, where people see more than a little of one another, usually they have been linked before. The two egos, through evolution, have to come together to work through certain phases for their benefit.'

'Shall I be able to remember any of my lives?'

'To remember depends upon your development.'

With regard to helping others, in response to a question, he said, 'It is no good presenting Truth to those who have no eyes to see. And those who have eyes to see will get it from within themselves.'

'It is no good then, trying to teach and help?'

'It is a great deal of good.'

'I don't wish to progress only for myself, I want to be allowed to help others.'

'That would be a waste, would it not? No, you shall help, but first you must prove your own steps.'

'Once you said to me that "when two vibrations are in harmony one with another no misunderstanding between them is possible". Well, after a while I dared to think that you might have spoken thus to indicate that – should I presume to think my own vibration in harmony with a fraction of yours – that no misunderstanding is possible between us. Was I right?'

I was aghast at my temerity.

'Yes, your subsequent thoughts were right. If it were not so, do you think I could contact you? And now, my child, I must give this child back her body. God bless you. Goodnight.'

And he was gone.

A few minutes later the two men walked in.

One more interview was recorded.

March 9, 1942:

'Once more he came, when Pippa and I were alone in her little sitting-room.

' "Well, my dear child?" ' he said with serene ambience.

'I felt relaxed and soothed by his presence and I sat silent, feeling there was no need for words between us.

'Then he leaned forward and said, "In this fashion we must use words. Pippa would never forgive us if we just sit and stare at one another!" (For I report to her something of what is said.)

'Struggling with the happiness that had lately filled me was an incredulity at the immensity of some of his words. I was like those whom I condemn who cannot believe a thing "because it is too good to be true".

'After some conversation he spoke of Pippa's health.

' "Will you try to persuade her to have her eyes looked at. They are badly inflamed at the back. Even now I can feel the pain in them. She got some stuff in a bottle and blithely diagnosed her own case as a little conjunctivitis – but it is not that. There are some days when she can hardly see. She must have expert advice. If something is not done she may even lose her sight. You need not tell her this, of course, but she must have them seen to."

'While he was talking he treated the eyes with the fingertips. I promised to see that she went to an oculist.

'I then asked an unrecorded question.

'He said, "It would not help you to know more about me, or That which sent me."

' "How can I learn more about That which sent you?"

' "Through yourself."

'I looked at him, seeking to draw his thoughts from him. Then I asked a question which I thought would draw forth a long and detailed explanation.

' "Yes," he said briefly.

' "Only yes?"

' "Yes. Yes is an affirmative. Do you want more?"

' "Yes, a good deal more!"

' "My dear child, you must work these things out by referring to your own wisdom. You should prove your own mettle."

' "Oh, I don't like this system of rationing!" I wanted from him long explanations and dissertations. But that was not his plan. He would provide only pointers, I must do the rest myself.

' "Rationing is in force all over the world at present! We must conform," he smiled.

'I learned from him not so much by what was said, but as it were, by contagion. The pupil learns from contact with the master's thought more than by his dissertations. And above all I knew that he was there, available, and would scold or correct me orally if I were at fault.

'After a while I asked a question about the power of the ego.
'"To have great power means to be able to receive great power. There is no evil power as such – where this sort of thing seems to result it means that something is wrong with the receiving set. The great power is being used in the wrong way."
'We talked about Pippa's doubting habit of mind. He said, "An extremely rare thing might happen. The intellect may pull her through. As intellects go it is of the first water." And as he spoke he stroked her forehead murmuring: "Peace, peace."
'"Shall I tell her that?"
'"You may – but she will not believe you!"
'A little later I said something which I thought needed further elucidation, "I mean...." I said.
'"My dear child, you know that I know exactly what you mean."
'"Can you read all my thoughts?"
'"The mind of man is so subterranean a structure that it would take a lifetime to explain it."
'"I find it so difficult to know my own footling mind."
'"No more footling than the stars," he said quietly.
'Later I asked about his expression "an old soul".
'"Souls are leaving group consciousness and arriving in this world to take the shape of man, dying and so leaving it again, every minute of the twenty-four hours. Some have been men longer than others."
'"And does the soul of man have to come only through the ape?"
'"No."
'"It seems a big jump from a horse or a dog to a man."
'"Why? As I said before, they both have two legs, two arms, and a head. Is it so very different? Other faculties are added as man increases his capacity, his stature."
'"Oh." I was thoughtful. "That explains the eyes of some men. Though I suppose there is a very considerable jump in time – in thousands of years perhaps – between the dog, and the man or woman one is likely to meet. Does the newly-arrived man only appear in the backward races?"
'"By no means. They appear in the white races too. But they are, of course, in the early stages of society." And he added, "Just as unicellular life divides to form, to let through new life,

so throughout all life, cells are giving birth to more cells, more life, more souls, more egos."

' "A sweet-working law."

' "Yes, it is a sweet-working law."

'I asked a question about "the stuff people are made of".

' "Everyone is made of the same stuff – God." And he spoke of the ties which hold people to one another through time and space, the ties of love.

' "Remember also what I said to you earlier as to the magnetic workings of the law of heredity; men are born to the parents they either merit or deserve."

' "I see. I cannot understand how a nation maintains its national characteristics if people of different nationalities pass through reincarnation."

' "I have just answered that question. However, there is really no such thing as a national characteristic, except that which is determined by parental influence and climatic conditions. It is a nation of individuals."

' "But how does national Karma work in this?"

' "You must not forget, as we said, that no one reincarnates into a body that he has not earned or deserved through Karmic Laws."

' "I see. So that according to his Karma, a man reincarnates into that nation which will help him to go through certain experiences."

' "Exactly."

' "It seems to me," I said, speaking of that which I have for so long felt, "that there is a steel rod of Truth which underlies and upholds all things, and that is the Law. And if only one could put it clearly into words, into teaching, people would understand life so much better."

' "Call it a steel rod of Truth if you like. The rod or spine is behind all things, but it cannot be put into words. There are many facets to the rod of Truth. What is Truth to a man at one stage of his evolution is not Truth to him at another." He paused. "You do see that, don't you?"

' "Yes – I see that."

' "And now, my child, I must leave you. Remember what I say, always keep your feet upon the ground. There is much to be learned from the world and from men."

' "But I want to learn about the stars."
' "You will learn about the stars. But remember Icarus. Also do not become too mind conscious. It is not an intellectual exercise, you know!"
'Then I said, "You have given me such great happiness – I wish I knew what I could give you."
' "I am glad. You could not have received if you had not given. And now, my child, this is not of course farewell. God bless you." '

Chapter Nine
MOUNTAIN SLOPES

By this time my wings were beginning to be fledged.

During the practice of the Silence I found that I was able to come up towards the rooftops of the skyscraper of the human edifice and was at last beginning, however haltingly, to look around. With the care and direction of the master-hand behind me, certain experiences came my way.

I learned much that was above the level of words. By pictorial means, by flashes of vision as well as a real experiencing, my Mentor-in-Spirit showed me how things are.

In the folds of Eternity all things are possible, and a little probing human mind can only apprehend reality in accordance with its own capacity to receive and understand. In those times when my consciousness was freed from the physical vehicle, and struggling upwards upon flights of exploration, he – as it were – took me by the hand and showed me round.

He had already taught that like vibration attracts like vibration, and consequently the experiences which began to come to me were not of the sort that might be afforded a psychic investigator into the realms of human existence immediately beyond the earth plane. I took these for granted. What was of deeper interest to me was an exploration of the metaphysical forces of Light which were the essence of the planes beyond and of our own world and living.

Often I used the hours of the night for experimentation as my days were busy. For many hours I would lie in what the Teacher called a 'cataleptic trance' while he discoursed with me, and answered my questions or led my thought into planes where elucidation was given as a kind of experience. It seemed as though I became one with Reality and would experience the forces which in their cause and effect provided the weave of existence. The perception reached in this sort of meditation was like the opening of a spiritual centre in the head, the escape of the spirit into further dimensions, so that one lived what one saw. One knew oneself to be a part of the forces of being. And ever after, if I wished to understand a living problem I would try to refer it to those conditions of being in order to find out how the law worked. Thus I began to understand the Laws of Living, limited ever by my own capacity to receive and interpret.

I found that to understand one must experience Reality in one's own soul, as well as have an intellectual acceptance of it.

I give these details, as it may be that they will help others who are struggling up the same thorny track.

I found that in this state, while I could hear and converse easily with the Teacher, and even unite sufficiently with his mind faintly to perceive what he wished to show me, I was still acutely aware, if I thought about it, of what was going on around me. Noises in the house or in the road outside, the milkman calling or footsteps around the house, were registered with greater clarity than was normal.

In this state I found it hard to move a muscle. The body seemed to be rigid, the limbs like lead. Force of will could move them or shift my position, but it was an effort.

Tremendous heat flooded through the body in this condition and often I would lie in a welter of perspiration.

All these small technicalities seemed to be a part of the exercise, but as I knew no-one with whom I could discuss what I was about, I was not able to discover if these symptoms were usual or in order. But I had implicit faith in my Teacher, and he dangled many a celestial carrot before my most human nose.

I remember once, when in the 'higher condition' I must have been lagging badly, for he suddenly flashed what seemed like a torchlight full into my mind. It was such a shock that I exclaimed aloud and this caused me to tumble down the slippery heights. But the memory of that flash availed me often, when the darkness was heavy around me; it gave me a point of light to visualize.

I found the truth of the words: 'For as much as without Thee we are not able to please Thee. . . .'

If we have no light in the mind we cannot reach the supernal Light. We must create the Light by the power of imagination in order to hold the wavelength in our minds which will cause the in-flash of the celestial Lightning.

Thus does a Master teach his pupil. By this and many other means.

Music was often used. If I was depressed and low, heavy to lift, a bracing melody would permeate my mind, a Mozart concerto, some passages of Beethoven, a fugue of Bach, or even the merry jingle of a light musical air. To illustrate the deep undertone of faith which is needed to support life, very special music was needed, and this would be caused to pound with inevitable majesty through my mind. To lift depression, or to kindle a sense of humour, to make one cease to take oneself too seriously, to laugh at oneself, jocular songs were used, in whose lines there were pertinent words to tease or chide me, or whose lilt was renewing or sweet.

As time went on the Teacher led me through certain experiences which were illustrative of the planes beyond. The first actual experience of this sort is recorded in my journal upon March 1, 1942:

'I was fully awake and practising the mind's powers. Suddenly I was carried up through space. In the parentheses of my mind I knew that my body was propped upright still on the cushions, and that a wrench would once more drag my focus of consciousness back into the body. But now I was free.

'Then I found myself in a land of splendid sunshine. I was on a shoulder of a celestial and shimmering mountain. Behind and below me were unfathomed depths of Space flowing out deep and wide into Eternity; to the right the mountain sloped downwards steeply and to the left its crystal slopes rose upwards, till it faded beyond my vision into the essence of Light.

'Around the fringe of the ledge on which I stood were flowers and I wondered how they grew and were nourished, for there was no soil as we know it. The ground seemed to be made of some sparkling substance like crystal. Most predominant were blue flowers like gentians, a deep and regal blue, and I looked into their little trumpets and felt refreshed. There were white flowers too, low on the ground, like daisies, only with larger petals; and each of them seemed to have a little face, though I distinguished no features, just a point of radiation in each centre. I knew that a loving emanation glowed up from each. I thought that yellow crocuses would look nice among them, and tried to create and affix some there with my mind, but they would not stay, and melted as soon as thought of. I supposed I was not thinking with sufficient strength and skill.

'Then I saw that standing on the shoulder of the mountainside was he whom I had come to visit, our "Friend in God". And I knew that I was here in answer to my burning wish that I might go with him, to stand a little while behind him, but still with him who was my Teacher, on the fringe of the place where the Christ Light might be known.

'I could not see face or features. Yet he was in human form. Perhaps he had assumed it to please me, I thought, for I did not think he usually used it. I saw sandalled feet and folds of a long robe, a sort of toga style, with one corner thrown over the shoulder. His hands were stretched out towards me.

'I put my fingers into his and tried to look at him. I could feel rather than see his smile, and a quick glance at his eyes of light caused me to drown . . . in memory. It was as though the interior of his mind was like a cathedral, and all about it were side chapels, and each chapel was the fullness of a life on earth.

'I think we spoke a little, but what was said I do not know; much thought was communicated without words.

'Then I noticed that I was clad in a loose garment, white, which was draped from the shoulders and gathered fully at the waist like a Greek robe.

'Then he led me towards the ascending mountain slope. Together we mounted the sparkling way.

'I was surprised to find that no effort was needed to make so steep an ascent. It seemed as though the vibration of my "Friend in God" was spread around me as a cloak, supporting me, carrying me upwards.

'We ascended blithely.

'First we passed through what I called to myself a rainbow belt. These were flowery places, flowers growing from the crystal ground. And as we went I noticed that some of the great translucent rocks were of ruby, amethyst, topaz; they were mountains of pure colour, rocks which shone like the jewels that they were.

Everywhere the atmosphere was light, our bodies were weightless, and our footsteps scarcely touched the ground.

'Then we rose to more lofty slopes, and came to a realm of pure light. Here there was no colour, rather a suffused glow, opalescent, radiant, with a soft pearly sheen.

'A magnificent joy was in the air. It *was* the air.

'Then we left this exalted altitude, mounting ever higher upon the wings of thought until we came to a place near the invisible, unimaginable Peak of the Holy Mountain. It was the limit of our attainment, the bounds of our – or rather my – ability to ascend. All things were left behind that were form. Here there was no colour, no flowers, only light.

'We were bathed in its brilliance, in its scintillating joyousness.

'Here we halted.

'Ahead of us, obscuring all else, was a mighty Focal Point of Light.

'Here was no form, no localized Being. Here was Glory.

'The radiance showered as a cascade about me. Ever afterwards I used the memory of that gentle sparkling fall as an exemplar of "the hem of that holy garment". In dark times on earth it gave me a focus and a vision of those illustrious Heights.

'My Companion was beside me, knowing and sharing what I felt.

'I do not know how long we stood there, transfixed in ecstasy.

'Then we backed away, turned and seemed to fly down the iridescent mountainside, so filled were we with reflected radiance that the feet did not touch the sparkling ground. We passed through the places of colour, of flowers. And then at last we came once more down to the little platform on the mountainside.

'We faced one another, and I knew that we must separate.

'I remember no words.

'Then I suddenly found myself falling. . . .

'In panic I struggled to get back to that bright Mountain of Light, but it was of no use. I fell on down into the vaporous mists below, mists that grew thicker and darker as I fell. I felt the earth coming up to meet me. I could feel its tug. It was pulling me back – and down.

'Then I landed in my body at home.

'I was weeping and hugging my body in a sickening pain which tore at the solar plexus.'

On another occasion, when I visited that place, words were spoken, or rather wafted towards me as a breath of wind formed into speech.

The first part of the experience was similar. We met as before upon the shoulder of the mountain in that spicy atmosphere which was so intoxicating in its lightness and fragrance. I saw the flowers, and the jewel-like rocks. We sped with effortless steps up to the vantage point of worship. I stood again beside my Companion and basked in that ineffable Radiance.

As before, I was enraptured with the glory of the Holiness which radiated intense power and love from that central Theme. One's being was bathed in and emptied of all but light.

It was as though we stood once again within the 'Hem of His Garment', embraced in His beams.

When we had regained our plateau I said to my Companion, 'I cannot keep up this altitude today. May we go somewhere a little less exalted?' I was feeling melted by the intense acceleration of power.

He took me down to the land of nature, to the heavens of natural life and humanity. We stepped over the edge of the mountainside, as it were, and I saw near below that the steep slopes were covered with daffodils. As we trod down among them there were carpets of primroses too, tufted and starry, each radiating as from a tiny personal being.

Then we reached a little valley. Here was a small open greensward, while away to my right I was aware that the land contrived to fall steeply away through deep gorges towards the normal planes of Earth which seemed to be many miles below.

I knew that were I to allow it the clutch of Earth would pull me back.

And while he stood by, I fell on my knees to kiss the sweet ground. It was unbelievably lovely, covered with starry mosses, and studded with tiny flowers whose faces shone like smiling jewels. The sward was bounded on one side by trees, and here were animals, here were birds. They were mingling together in freedom and an exhilarating joyousness.

Then I turned and saw a waterfall, torrenting down over

crystal rocks and flowing merrily on in a stream which wound down through the valley and was lost among trees and distance. Over the waterfall hung a single tree, luminous with abounding life.

Exclaiming in delight, I went to the waterfall and, garmented as I was, stepped into the water. I let it cascade over me, but it did not make me wet. I felt the sparkling drops of water on face and body, refreshing me, but it did not make me wet. When I stepped again onto the bank I shook drops from me, and every crystal drop seemed alive.

Then it was time to leave.

Together we sailed up again to the mountain plateau. This time I begged him to accompany me back.

'It hurt so much last time,' I said.

And even as I spoke Earth memories pulled and I was falling. But this time he was with me. His presence supported me like wings.

We approached the Earth gradually. I looked down and saw the closing mists below. Over the oceans it was lighter, and over the poles, quite light. But over the populated and warring parts of Earth there hung a thick yellowish fog. Then suddenly the atmosphere changed and lightened somewhat. My consciousness jerked and shifted its focus – I was sitting at home – and the light was the sunlight of a March day.

For ever afterwards I knew that to reach that Holy Light one did not have 'to go' anywhere. Wherever one was, was THAT, to be contacted if one could achieve intunement.

I had learned that the creative power of the mind was in its own essence divine, and through visualization of the pitch desired the mind naturally and necessarily takes on something of the quality of the concept envisaged.

I learned to understand the value of the 'Jesus story'. I saw how superb an object lesson it was. How it provided Western people with a focal point around which they could build their vision – and their intunement.

I had learned also that there comes a point in the spiritual development of a man when he must leave the purely human vision of Jesus, leave the carpenter's son, forget his humble birth, and even the holy dying, and see only the transfigured and transcendental Essence of the Divine.

I had learned that that which we call 'God' is a Radiance which comes to us from the Most High, the First Cause, showering to us like the sun's rays. Each unit of the Radiance is a rudiment of Mind, containing the qualities of life, mind and consciousness. . . . That living things grow by absorbing this Radiance upon many levels. And that because we are made of this God-stuff, we use ourselves in little as He in great.

Chapter Ten

DARKNESS

The next journey with my Teacher was of quite another kind. It took me into realms unpermeated by any light.

I quote my journal, dated March 19, 1942 :

'I was in a place of darkness, with him beside me, knowing what was toward.

' "They are on you! Fight!" cried the Voice I was so used to hearing.

'Suddenly I was aware that I was being attacked, sprayed with poisonous energies; my body was being forced to clamour with the poisons of desire, making it opaque, chaining it to the rock of heavy wants.

'I knew I must fight. I was smothered and weighed down. All the weights of Hell were on me, pulling me downwards, always down. My body was nothing but a furnace. Through this the inner "me", the observer, detached, looked on and willed the fight. Foul shadows surrounded me, polluting and polluted, while I strove to beat off their vile menace. At that moment it seemed as if I must be engulfed, that I must be drawn down suffocating, submerged by hellish powers. But I strove still to fight. The shadows formed shapes, crude, ugly shapes as of humans not quite human. They breathed their force upon me and their breath was horror and death.

'Gradually, with all the power I could command, and as though I were lifting an intolerable weight, I forced my thought up and out of this burden and pain.

'I tried to hold the vision of a radiant Cross.

'Close, closer must I bring it. With all the force of my will must I drag it to me. It must be my shield.

'I called upon the Christ aid.

'I called to the Most High.

'Yet still the devils clung, and nothing seemed to stay their pressing weight. Their multitudes came on, loathsome, forceful, pressing still upon me. I cried on the Christ for help.

'Then I thought of the child I used to be who would sing against all fears and so banish terror. And so I sang. Opening my lungs to that poisoned air, I sang.

'The Light grew steadier. I found that I could hold it more easily.

'The onslaught lessened. I dragged and strained at the White Light from On High, and flooded myself with its shining. I tried to make a pool of Light in which to stand, a pool of purity. The circle held, though the devils leaped across and preyed on me still, but their attacks were weaker. Then I made of myself a wheel. I forced the Light into a wheel of blazing swords about me. I was the hub; around me blazed an incandescence formed of whirling swords.

'Now I could fight with force. The evil fell back. The Light was winning.

'I lengthened my spears of light, I made the circle wider. Ever did I call upon the Light to stay with me, to encompass and protect me. And still I sang. It was to the air of the Chorale from Beethoven's Ninth Symphony. What words I invented to march with the measure of that grand melody, I have since forgotten. The essential was that Light was now showing. The jibbering fiends seemed further away. The air was lightening and I could breathe without suffocation. At last I could take my bearings and see something of the manner of the place I was in. It was a wide dark plain and behind me was the very base of a mountain. I backed towards it. Not yet was victory complete. I must draw more light for the defence, with weapons made of my own thought. I could feel the Light above me, and the lowering straining devils all around. I mounted a few paces backwards, my shafts of light still flailing, my song still quelling. I gathered all my force, such of the force of Christ that I could use, and sprayed it out before me into that poisonous lower air. I gathered confidence and hurled my very boredom of their wiles towards them. They backed away. I could breathe more slowly now, my feet were a little above their level. I was mounting towards the saving Light.

'Then suddenly I felt their tragedy. My heart yearned towards them. Inevitably as it seemed, my feet followed, and I stepped down again, away from the Light.

'Then I prayed and tried to spread my love among them. I sought to carry my song into the midst of them.

'Meanwhile the circle of light was widening round me, and the dark things were receding from it. Spraying them with love yet must I force them back, for they must be gone. I could not leave while they were here. I tried to sweep the plain with the force of Love using it as a shower, an emanation, and the heavy lowering wall of the dark multitude melted fast away and at last faded over the bleak horizon. But before they were quite gone I caught at one of them. I would teach them something, I thought, give them something of the Light to take back into their dusky haunts. It was a sort of pigmy that I had in my clutch, a small dusky thing. I caught it by its mop of black and wiry hair. And then I tried to show it beauty. "See," I said, "let us lighten this place. Do you know what is beauty, what it can do? See, these we call flowers, buttercups." And with my will I thought a scattering of the golden flowers. They shone around my feet.

'The little smoky thing in my grasp looked.

' "Pick some," I encouraged. "Take them with you and show them to the others."

'I watched it bend its crooked back, hoping as it touched the flowers that my thought had made them strong enough to last.

'As it ran off with its shining booty I felt a surge of tenderness towards it.

' "Take them, child," I called after it. "Take them with love."

'Then a doubt assailed me. Could this be real?

'The Voice said, "As real as you or I."

'And then I mounted home.

'A mortal weariness fell upon me.

' "I have wanted that weariness for thee," said the Voice.

'I felt almost lifeless, too weary to know the Light had won, too weary to rejoice at it.'

Chapter Eleven
THE RAYS

1

After some months of such teaching, of learning by living, and much effort and struggle, I began to develop more subtle and steady means of probing into the planes of the Beyond. I began to feel more sure. My budding intuitive antennae developed a more selective penetration, and through deeper experience I began to feel more certain of the waters in which I moved. I was taught to recognize instantly radiations from a debased or negative source, and how to protect oneself from them. Just as the sun's rays dry up swamps, so does the Divine Light clear away shadows.

In May 1942 I began once again to write the book, *The Wisdom of the Spirit*, this time sure that I was writing under guidance. Still ignorant of much that I wished to discuss in the book, I gave myself up to the Silence and wrote in a state of contemplation.

Once more I asked the question, 'I feel that there is a steel rod of Truth which underlies all things, that if one could uncover it, lay it bare, all things would be made understandable with reference to it. Is there such a rod of Truth?'

Then I paused and waited for an answer. In the first stage the answers came one by one as clearly formulated sentences.

'Call it a steel rod if you like. There is a spine to the body of Truth which constitutes our life, but it cannot be put into words. The most we can do is to try to put before our mind's eye a picture, woven in semi-metaphorical language, that will help us to visualize and understand the workings of the Laws of God; to try to understand those aspects of the Laws of God as they affect us in our tiny corner of the Cosmos. But at best our understanding must be small because of the limitation of our minds.'

'I would like to dig beneath the surface of things, to find out the theory of music which underlies the whole giant harmony. But the symphony is so vast. Where can we begin?'

'Contemplate the Rays.'

The words were incisive. I laid down my pen and did as I was bid. I probed into this thought. I contemplated the Rays. And swiftly my mind was caught up and I saw what was meant by 'the Rays'. Gradually I saw build up before my eyes a whole 'philosophy of the Rays'. And I saw that it made sense of all perplexities.

Thus did I begin to work at and expand my own understanding of this vast 'theory of music'. Throughout the whole of that book I asked the questions simply and as they occurred to me in my struggle for understanding, and the answers poured into my mind. Usually the answers were not given in the form of words. That which was taught me was given in flashes of knowing, or vision, in a state above the level of words. Often there were no words to describe what I perceived. And this difficulty has pursued me ever since, causing me nearly to split my brains in the effort to clothe in words the ideas offered.

The concept of the Rays I found made understanding miraculously simple.

I learned that the Rays are strands of radiation issuing from the innermost Source, the Ultimate. They are stepped down in force, in brilliance, or more technically, in frequency, from the Hub of the Wheel which is the First Cause, the Point of their inception, out towards the perimeter, the rim of the Wheel that contains all the Universes – both of Spirit and of matter.

These Rays, on their outward journey from the Mind of the Most High, lose power and perfection, and on the perimeter they weave into the physical things we know, stars, suns and earth.

Thus do the Divine Rays create and sustain as a continuous act, all the worlds. They are as the Spokes of the Wheel of Creation, the Hub is the very Mind of the Most High. It is this factor which gives life and mind and the eternal Core of Spirit to all living things. Conversely, as the Rays recede into the depths of the many-dimensional Wheel, they carry within them and weave the structure of the realms above, the Universes of Spirit. The journey from the perimeter towards the Central Sphere of the Divine is the purpose and goal of all life.

This is a way of expressing the inexpressible.

The Rays were shown to me as strands of many differing types of energy, as are the rays of the sun, of many varying shades, tones, colours and textures. They are as sheaths, holding within themselves many dimensions of refining energies, the outer creating physical things, the inner giving those of the Spirit. Each Ray contains an aspect of the Divine Mind. They build the elements in their many levels. Therefore each atom holds within it a rudiment of mind.

Life is a product of a complexity of the Ray-energies, whose inner levels are the Spirit. I had found the reason for the likeness in the limbs and organs throughout the animal and human world. Each was woven of a pattern of energies drawn from one or other of the same elements of creation, the Prime Rays. The radiations of the Divine Mind gave their quality and form to natural growth. All were spun upon the same archetypal energies.

The White Ray of Divine Light which holds all Fires, all qualities within It is called the 'Word', the Creative Lord, the Holy Logos.

To describe this vision in words is an impossible task. Who shall see with his understanding a sunset if, blind, he can only hear its description in words?

Yet sometimes instruction was given me in actual words. The sentences were dropped into my mind like snowflakes whose crystal patterns were formed in an upper realm.

'All growth is from within – outwards. First the etheric form within, then the physical expression of itself in matter.'

'But for what purpose?'

'Because God is creating out of His own substances, through experience, individuals potentially like Himself.'

This was the gist of that first book. And as I wrote, I learned from what my pen was writing.

In a fortnight the script was finished, and I had to turn my mind to the matter of its publication.

2

The war was still on. London was suffering under its worst bombing attacks. Exeter itself had just been the recipient of the first so-called 'Baedaker' raids. On this occasion the raid was more spectacular than destructive. It was a comparatively simple matter in those bright moonlight nights to navigate high over the silver strip of the Exe Estuary towards the City. Thousands of incendiary bombs were unloaded, but by some error of judgement they missed the centre of Exeter and were strewn along the western slopes of the hills. But we knew they would come again.

On May 2nd they did, this time decimating the centre of the city.

My eight-year-old son said it was the happiest night of his life!

Our house was a mile or so out of the city centre, on the hills to the north, and our midnight picnic in the kitchen and our singing to drown the din, in which our Sealyham joined, was considered by my son as a special treat.

It was in this setting and under these disadvantages that I was to set out to publish a book which would certainly be without popular appeal.

Tired of struggling in a waterless, gasless kitchen, I took train to Pippa, whose kitchen had both.

I hoped for an interview with my Teacher. To my way of thinking several suitable occasions presented themselves. Pippa sat peacefully with her knitting, my son practised the piano in the other room, and I tried to read patiently.

But I waited in vain.

When this happened again on a subsequent visit I was discomposed. In spite of the now fluent communication which had been established between my mind and his, I still was weak enough to long for the comfort of the human voice speaking to my human ear from the planes beyond. But I was to learn that my personal wish had no place in these austere realms.

That autumn, when Pippa was once more staying in Devon with us, and she and my husband and I were sitting around the fire, suddenly the longed-for Visitor shone his presence through our room.

I apologized for 'making a fuss' in the secrecy of my own mind, at his non-appearance months before.

'You have learned a lesson,' was all he would comment.

Fortunately the precious notebook was at hand, and my husband prepared to record the conversation. The first question was from him and concerned the difference between organic and inorganic matter. A detailed answer ensued. This led to further discourse upon the nature of the atom and kindred subjects. He spoke of the 'unbelievable rapidity of motion in the particles of the atom', and said that 'there will be invented in time an instrument which might be called a "perceptor" which will be able to gauge and register these things'.

We asked if there were life on the other planets.

'Life as you and – no, I cannot say I – as you know it, is only possible where certain conditions prevail. But it is possible for there to be life in other forms even where there is no atmosphere.'

We then fell to discussing a subject which had been puzzling us in those war-tortured years.

My husband asked if a man could inflict pain upon another beyond his deserts.

'Most decidedly not,' was the answer. 'No man can receive that which he has not earned. It is simply a matter of cause and effect.'

'Well,' said Wystan, 'might I not get hold of a man and torture him as much as I like, telling him that everything he gets he thoroughly deserves?'

Our Mentor smiled. 'You would probably find that he had a strong right arm and would impose a little Karma on you, or something would certainly intervene.'

Wystan was thinking of the current tales of the Nazi concentration camps. 'But there have been cases where a man has been able to torture others with impunity – if these tales are true.'

'They are true. But always there is the working of cause and effect. Such a man usually gets what he has deserved. When I say "deserved" I do not mean it in the sense of reward and punishment. There is no such thing. It is the working of the Law of Cause and Effect. And the torturer deserves our pity for he certainly will have to suffer as he had meted out to others.' He paused. Then, 'There comes a point in cases of extreme pain where compensation sets in.' On this he would say no more.

I then asked, 'Are all animals potential humans?'

'Yes, indeed.'

'And all insects too?'

'And all insects too. You will remember what I said about creatures belonging to a group consciousness.'

We talked about the higher animals, apes, dogs and horses.

'Do they nevertheless maintain their individual egos?'

'That is correct. Within the group consciousness individuality is preserved.'

And the discourse continued upon the subject of desire and its possible sublimation.

Then I said, 'Perhaps you will answer a practical question. So often I sit watching the sea birds as they curvet about. Why do birds wheel together as one? Is there a telepathy between them?'

'It is a kind of telepathy, that being the only word available to use. Like men they have a head, a leader. They follow him. They feel the vibration of his turn on the air and all act together – almost as one.'

'Beautiful, isn't it!' I said.

'As beautiful as a little child learning to walk,' he murmured.

And so our session came to an end. These occasional talks were a steadying factor in my development of thought. Had the Teacher wished to say more, outside the realms of my own mind, to correct or reprove me, he could do so through this means.

Chapter Twelve
SEEING

Between that time and February 1943 our Teacher came to us on several more occasions, sometimes when my husband was present and sometimes when he was not available. In these cases I wrote down afterwards from memory all that I could recall as it took place. But as time went on we used this outward, tangible method of speech in a manner that was less and less possible to report. Our conversations tended to carry on thoughts which had been broached and threshed out in the Silence, so that a listener would have found it hard to follow. While the rest was of a purely personal nature.

By this time it was clearly evident that my mind was able to tune in with his fluently, for thought and conversation between us in the Silence became as immediate and lucid as he had promised it would be. So now a physical mediumistic instrument was no longer necessary as a go-between. I will therefore give some fragments from the recorded notes which close this period of my life, for before the celestial Visitor used this method again, thirteen long years were to pass.

I was staying with these friends in September 1942. We were sitting in the little morning room. Pippa was busy at her typewriter. It was late afternoon and a grey light came in at the windows. I sat on the sofa with a book.

Suddenly the typing ceased. Glancing up I saw that the Teacher had taken over there and then, as she was at work. He stood up, eyes closed as usual, turned to me and gave the Sign. Then he picked his way through the furniture towards an armchair near to me. This he turned so that it faced me and sat down.

Though I was beginning to be used to his unorthodox methods, they were inclined to take my breath away.

I said, 'You are terrifyingly efficient.'

'That is wisdom,' was the lofty reply.

While I had been sitting with my book on my lap, ostensibly reading, I had been thinking about this Being who sometimes came to us. I was wondering about the lives he had led on Earth before he had gained his permanent release. While I sat thinking, the air had warmed, as it were, and a power had filled the room; and gradually a golden sheen of light, as of a yellow silken damask had spread through the atmosphere. In spite of the clacking of the typewriter, Pippa's turned back and the gloom outside, I was elated, electrified by this sudden lustre which filled the room.

Now he sat in the armchair, an august presence, and spoke no word.

I, taking my lead from him, also remained silent, wondering as to the reason for his visit.

For a whole hour we sat thus, and no word was spoken. And as I gazed at that serene countenance, gradually the face altered. It seemed as though this Visitor from another world was altering the bone formation of Pippa's face, or using energies which were supernatural in order to form other faces, superimposed over hers. Gradually the texture of the face changed. Her normally pale skin faded and I saw a ruddy masculine visage, weather-browned as men are not nowadays; it was tanned as if by horse-riding in all weathers. I saw a royal countenance of lofty brow, broad lineaments, strongly marked eyebrows, full round eyes, and a firm yet sweet expression about the mouth. The hair had a ruddy hue and was worn clubbed below the ears.

Then, as I watched spellbound, the face changed somewhat. I saw features which appeared to me to be foreign, perhaps from the Mediterranean basin, yet withal, strangely familiar. There were the same broad brow and jaw and cheek bones, the same full eyes. The head was nearly bald, and the whole aspect of a genial yet stern expression held the features. The skin was of a darker tan even than before.

Then once again the kaleidoscope of etheric forces melted and changed. This time another face formed, of a gentler and sweeter mien. Always the bone formation was similar, the long head (far higher and larger than that of Pippa), the arched brows, but this time the hair was chestnut, brisk and curling, swept back from the high forehead, with deep bays on either side of the centre of the brow. The face was wise and kind and humorous, with a dash of the debonair, and there was a neatly trimmed beard.

Other faces were shown me, too. I lost count. Usually I saw no accompanying dress or style of clothing. My eyes were wretchedly limited in their ability to see into this dimension, and constantly I altogether lost the spectacle which was being presented to me, and then Pippa's familiar much smaller physiognomy would suddenly show through these larger, more dramatic and powerful masks.

Once I exclaimed with exasperation at my own limitation. 'Yes, but they don't *set*!' I cried, when the pictures seemed to melt and then form again. I longed for a much clearer and more fixed vision, for at best these were but fleeting glimpses. But they were real and true, of that I was certain. They were being forced through the ether by a concentrated and intense effort of creative thought, by the master-mind. I was privileged to watch this cineramic presentation of certain of the identities which our Teacher had used on Earth. As yet I did not know the names of these dynamic-looking men. All the while that he was with me on that occasion the golden sheen of light persisted, hanging like a gauze of luminous yellow silk throughout the room.

Then as suddenly as he had come, he said, 'Farewell' and withdrew.

Pippa awoke, cross at having wasted so much time when she wanted to get on with her typing, and resentfully her subconscious dream mind threw out the words, 'Must wind up the clocks.' While I turned away, moved beyond words.

One day I sat in the higher condition of consciousness, without directing my mind toward any particular investigation. I was united in mental perception with my Teacher, and I waited passively to see what today's lesson would bring.

After a few minutes experiences began to open before my inner vision. I was walking along a dark corridor. At the end I discerned a flight of steps leading upwards. They were of wrought iron. At a little landing there was a door in a high wall. Up these steps I went until I reached the platform before the door, but then suddenly I found that my mind could not hold the necessary concentration. I fell back and was once more at the bottom of the flight of trellised steps. I caught hold of my mental focus and forced myself up those steps again. I must get through that door.

I knew that I should learn a lot if I could only open it. I struggled up the steps, but the mind was like an untamed horse, it jerked the rein from my grip and my focus withdrew; and I was back on the plane of earth again in my room at home.

A few days later I was there again, there was the corridor. I noticed as I went that the walls were blue. I came to the steps, and holding my mental concentration with what I thought was a grip of iron, I ascended the stairs. Once more I tried to reach that door. But my mind was weak and fluctuating. The experience would not hold, and shortly after, once more I was back again in the body.

On the third occasion I came to this place, this dimension, I saw that there were pictures on the blue walls of that long corridor. They were portraits.

'When you can hold this firmly you will be able to learn about the past,' said the Teacher.

Some weeks went by.

Then came a day when my mind must have been working strongly. Once more, in the higher concentration, I was taken to this sphere. I passed easily along the corridor, glancing at the portraits as I went, but I did not recognize the faces. I ascended the steps and to my delight pushed open the door in the wall.

At once I was in a garden filled with sunlight. It was in formal style, long lawns with lavender hedges in full bloom and flowers of all kinds. I walked up the central paved pathway, for at the end I espied a pavilion like a Greek temple. I knew with my innermost level of thought that only the most inflexible resolution would keep me here. I must hold myself here with my mind's focusing powers and refuse all slipshod tendencies to remember the earth plane.

I skirted a formal waterpool and ascended some broad steps up to the temple. As I walked I was appraising the material of which the steps were made. It was a pinkish alabaster.

Then my eye lighted on a sandalled foot and I looked up in astonishment.

There, seated on a curved Greek stool, was a figure in a long robe, a kind of white toga with a green border. The noble head was that of an old friend, this I knew, but I knew no name. Short, dark curls crowned the austere countenance and the expression was brilliant as sunshine.

Saying no word he got up and walked to the back of the pavilion. I followed. An arched entrance gave outwards onto a dusty road, with a white wall which ran diagonally along this lane. The sunshine was blazing and hurt the eyes as it reflected off that long white wall. We walked along the track together and I knew that inside that wall was a villa where many were gathered for spiritual studies and for dancing and other sports. But alas, my concentration broke before I could learn more.

On the next occasion when I came up those alabaster steps the stool was now a rough throne. On it sat waiting for me the same soul, a man of strength and dignity. This time he was wearing a rich apparel of russet brown with a broad studded belt and thonged leggings. The hair was the colour of rust and once again was short and curling. The fine countenance was bent towards me with a smile and I saw then that the eyes were full and grey and tender. His hand was held out towards me.

Many times I was conducted back to that Greek temple which formed an amphitheatre, a stage, for the meeting of people I had once known. Always I recognized and knew them, but only gradually was I taught to know their names.

This exercise was used as a method of strengthening the power of concentration, for the deep interest in the figures brought forth from the past helped to fix one's focus, and thus we could learn about our associates in the distant past.

By this time we knew that if the Teacher wished to come and speak with us through the vocal chords of Pippa he would come whether we were awaiting him or not. Not for him the dimmed lighting and bated breath of psychic sittings. He simply assumed control. It seemed that this was the wiser way in these circumstances. 'I have the knack of contacting,' he said simply, in way of explanation. Always he showed knowledge of whether we were likely to be disturbed by callers in the near future, or other events which might interrupt. Always he was seeking for methods of instructing me as to the working of the Laws of Living. So my powers of observation and assessment were continually on the stretch.

Once, when Simon and Wystan had gone out for a while together, leaving Pippa and me alone for the evening, she and I sat idly by the fire talking, and I could not help expecting and hoping for a visit from our Teacher. All the evening Pippa and

I chatted desultorily, but he did not come. I felt foolishly disappointed. But there were other plans in store.

That night I awoke sharply, as though someone had shaken me by the shoulder.

Startled, I sat up.

There, standing at the end of my bed, was an apparition of Fire.

This was not as when I was a child, the soft glowing sense of a Presence, seen with an inner knowing. This was a Figure of brilliance, though not of human form. A column of shimmering golden or orange fire, about the height of a tall man, was surmounted by a circle of radiant flame. It was like a great halo about two feet across of concentric rings of white and orange fire, and the centre was a lavender violet or blue. Beside me, out of the corner of my eye, I could just glimpse the copper-fire column of another such Figure. But I could not see the brilliant head for I did not dare to turn my eyes.

How long I remained gazing at these visitations I do not know, but when they vanished I lay down and slept once more. I knew that I had been shown beings in spiritual form such as a liberated man may use in the upper latitudes, when human bodily shape might be tedious and without usefulness.

Chapter Thirteen

PROGRESS AND PUBLICATION

1

Towards the end of 1943 I felt impelled to visit Pippa and Simon once more.

Things were far from well between them and I was anxious for their happiness.

It was a clash of temperaments which was hard to reconcile. Simon's powerful personality was a veritable Vesuvius which occasionally erupted. He was a captivating and vital personality, as stimulating as champagne, but such ebullience had a debit side which Pippa found irresponsible and exhausting. And so feathers flew. When I arrived the battle was at its height. Tempers were flaming. Pippa was acid, storming up and down, and finally Simon, white-lipped, stalked out of the house.

Then suddenly into this distraught atmosphere, the Teacher took over.

Pippa was made to cease her restless pacing up and down and to sit by the fireside. The trance condition was in full grip, the eyes were closed, the finger tips stroked the forehead and the lips murmured, 'Peace, peace'.

I realized forcibly the truth of what the Teacher had said to us earlier, that he had 'the knack of taking over'.

The sign of the Cross was made as usual.

I subsided into a chair. Once more I was impressed by the Teacher's power to dominate a situation and his total neglect of ceremony when need arose. The master rider collected the horse under him and disciplined the scattered potencies within the room.

Silence reigned.

Then he turned to me with a smile which signalled that we may now proceed.

Immensely relieved and comforted by the sudden calm after

the storm, I said, 'I was worried about them. Did I do right to leave everything at home and come?'

'My dear child, did you feel impelled to come?'

'Yes, I thought so.'

'Then you did right.'

'It is often so hard to judge one's motives. To know where one's duty lies.'

I knew by this time that this Teacher never ordered or commanded his protégés. They must make up their own minds upon every instance. Only hints were given, or gentle impulsions, never commands. And this is so to this day. The will is left entirely free.

'Do you think I am going to lay down hard and fast rules? You are an individual, you must make your own decisions in all cases. Do as your own wisdom dictates.'

Then he spoke of Pippa's health. He said that she was very depleted, and that 'Something is a little wrong inside. She may need another operation to put it right, but she must be stronger first.'

'The physical condition affects the nerves,' he continued, and then, 'These two grate on one another's subconscious a little at present. There are storms in teacups. But while one is in the teacup they seem very real, don't they!'

'Yes,' said I, 'but I like to remember that teacups are open to the sky.'

Then I commented upon the fact that I had not been able to persuade Pippa to have her eyes attended to.

'It does not seem to be very much use telling Pippa to do anything about her physical frame, does it!' He smiled tolerantly. 'She should have the treatment, however, but she takes but little notice of what I say, it seems.'

'She has not the pleasure of experiencing you, as one might say,' I answered, 'so she does not have our conviction.'

He looked at me quizzically with that look of subtle sweetness yet power that ever lit his presence.

'That you look on me as a person, I suppose is inevitable.'

'Are you not a person?' I asked.

'Do you not know the difference between a person and an individual?'

But I was still puzzled.

'My child,' he said, with whimsical emphasis on the word 'child'. 'Personality is the "you" within the body. It is determined partly by your physical make-up, physical conditions, glands and so on. The individual is the "I am". It is not attainable while in the body. And that is the last occasion on which I shall spoon-feed you!'

'And the individuality is a certain mixture of rays or vibrations?' Often I used to say things especially to draw him out.

'Your individuality is what you have made yourself. What you call a low vibration is not necessarily a wrong one, you know. The children of the first form are not more wrong than those in the sixth form. They are merely at a different stage of development.'

I mentioned the case of a friend who tended to find herself suddenly out of her body. 'Is there any value in these experiences?'

'There is little value in the ex-corpus experiences you mention. It is the result of what is known as a "loose etheric".'

'When one is out of the body what vibration does one contact?'

'That depends upon the vibration you have learned to contact.'

'And in the cases I have read of, of travelling across the world out of the body?'

'It is done very much more rarely than you would think, and the benefit of course is according to how the individual has learned to use the potentialities of the experience.'

Later on I asked, 'Is the significance of the Cross that of perfect balance?' I wished to get him to discuss it.

'Yes, the symbol of the Cross signifies perfect balance. But there is more than one significance. It is a very ancient symbol, more ancient than most of us realize. It originated with the earliest man, the head, the arms, the legs.'

'And perfection of balance is what we all are striving to achieve?'

'Perfection of balance is what all men are striving to achieve. All are on the path of Wisdom at one stage or another. Balance is Wisdom.'

'And what is Beauty?'

'Beauty is Wisdom.'

'And what is Light?' I wanted to make him talk, dilate and expand the concepts which had been pouring into my head.

'My dear Clarice, I can scarcely believe you are serious. That was said from the outer skin!'

'Oh!' I exclaimed. 'I feel like a chicken in the egg – I cannot see for the shell! And you, the mother chicken, are out in the light!'

He smiled. 'When I have got you out of the egg, I shall make a very neglectful parent.'

'Oh dear! What does that portend?'

'Too much mothering only weakens.'

I asked him about pain and joy, why the two are so much akin.

'They are both vibration intensified. Love and hate, pain and joy, one the bowl inverted, the other the bowl filled. Do you not see that it is the same thing?'

'I am finding it difficult,' I said, 'to hold a point of balance between the joy of life and the pain.'

'Yes, I know. It is a thing you must learn for yourself.' His brow furrowed.

I was silent for a while.

Then he said quietly, 'There are always growing pains.'

'At least there is comfort in that word "growing",' said I.

'I hoped you would draw some comfort from that.'

I asked a question which had been in the forefront of my mind in that violent period of *Blitzkrieg* and bombing attacks night and day.

'About accidents. Can one precipitate oneself into the next world before one's time? People who fall under buses, and so on?'

'Nothing can come to you that is not of your own making. What is called accident, what is called chance, are really two words which mean precisely nothing. Accident and chance do not exist. All is according to law, to cause and effect. You create your own circumstances. You know that perfectly well.'

'Yes, but I wanted to hear you say it aloud.'

'And my confirmation will do?'

'Of course.'

'You do me great honour,' he said.

'*I* could not do you sufficient honour,' said I.

He was silent.

Then, thinking of all this new knowledge, I blurted out, 'Death is a questionable catastrophe.'

He smiled. 'That is a questionable remark!'

'I mean that death viewed from one angle is calamity, yet not from another.'

'Why this preoccupation with death, my dear child?'

'I suppose because death has been very close around me just lately.'

'It is a good thing to remember that everything that comes to you is in the Path of your development. And death is really quite a long way off from you – from you and yours – taken in time, quite a long way off.'

'Thank you for saying that. It is comforting. But the flesh is so horribly weak.'

'It is always bound to appear so. Remember – have no fear. With peace and tranquillity, have no fear.'

I asked a question about the potentialities of prayer. I hoped he would give me a considerable discourse.

'Meditate upon it,' was all the answer he would give, and refused to be drawn further except to add, 'You know there is much which cannot be spoken through this method.'

I spoke of the difficulties which I sometimes experienced in the folds of the Silence in my inner consciousness.

'You have to learn to be focused, to stand alone, to be independent. I want to help you to be strong, to think for yourself.'

'I get in a panic sometimes, when I lose my way in the darkness.'

'What sort of evil thing should I be if I tried to possess your thought? I want to help you to think for yourself – to be *self*-possessed. The paths of Wisdom are not easy. There are snares, there are pitfalls, there are dangers and difficulties, there is panic and doubt. But,' his voice was resonant, 'there is courage, there is Light. I want you to know that you always have a friend who sympathizes, who loves you.'

'There is great comfort in that word *always*,' I said gratefully. 'And realization; does it consist of ever-ascending peaks?'

'You may put it that way if you like. But you must remember that every peak of realization has to be earned.'

There was an irresistible, beguiling delight in his presence. When he was there all seemed so safe, so hallowed, and I felt my heart expand under his serene affluence.

Later I asked a question which a friend had recently put to

me, 'Can a force of evil gather round a man and make him do an evil deed?'

'Looked at superficially – no. There must always be in the man an answering vibration which tunes in with the outside influence.'

Then I remembered how, during the previous night, while I lay wrestling with a particular problem that refused to clarify itself, I suddenly had seen the strongly formed picture held before my inner eye of a donkey struggling up a hill.

'I am sorry to make you work like a donkey!' I said, and he knew that I was referring to my perpetual questioning and my frequent recalcitrance in understanding.

'Donkeys have wills of their own, don't they?' he said.

'Wills like iron bars,' I answered. And we both reflected upon his firmness with me in the Silence, upon what he called his 'clubbings', the frequent (albeit gentle) scoldings, and his refusal any longer to make it easy for me; his insistence that I came at the answer to the problem in my own way, through hard work.

'But I like your clubbings,' I added. 'I feel safe with them.'

He said, 'And now bless you with all the beauties of heaven. You know that it is not necessary any longer to talk in this way.' Then briskly, 'Now this child will earn reprimand unless she gets on with things.'

And with the Sign he was gone.

Pippa awoke slowly and looked about her with surprise.

'Oh, I feel better,' she said. 'I suppose he's been! He gives me a feeling of rest and refreshment.'

Five minutes later some friends arrived to visit us.

2

By the time I had finished typing my book, *The Wisdom of the Spirit*, I wondered how I could find a publisher.

In this connection things happened in a way which demonstrates the 'celestial staff-work' that I had been so aware of on many occasions.

My Teacher had occasionally, in answer to a question, refused to give advice but had reiterated firmly, 'Do what you feel impelled to do.' And it was good to have in robust words which hit upon the outer ear that which had been the way I had tried to follow.

I knew my Mentor would not issue bald instructions upon so mundane a point as the search for a publisher, so I listened for the sense of impulsion. My book was obviously of limited appeal, which in peacetime would have been difficult enough to place, but now, with the London blitz raging, with almost every commodity scarce and paper in short supply, the outlook should have been hopeless.

However, by deft impulsions I came to hear of a man who published works of a spiritual nature. I wrote to him and subsequently sent him the manuscript.

The effect was electric. He telephoned me accepting the book and inviting me to an interview.

I went to London immediately. I found my publisher to be a man of knowledge and experience in the ways of the Spirit, who had written several books himself on esoteric subjects.

He startled me by saying that he recognized by the style of my book that 'a certain member of the celestial Hierarchy instructed me'. And to my astonishment he gave me those initials to designate the Teacher, which a few weeks before had hung in letters of fire nearly two feet high in the darkness of my room.

I felt like a winded athlete.

For years I had been groping along alone, unable to find anyone to speak to who would understand, because I supposed everyone would think me mad. Now here was a man who was not only familiar with this method of instruction from the Beyond, but who actually gave me the initials which I had been told by my Teacher represented the name he was known by in the esoteric world. I had read no esoteric books and had no notion at that time of the world of inner studies. Now this man claimed in fact that he recognized the teaching in my book and the style of writing. He said some generous things about the book and hastened to put in train the plans for its publication.

Here, if we needed it by this time, was proof of the subtle direction we were receiving from the Beyond.

The Wisdom of the Spirit came out in January 1943, so my new friend had made a pretty swift job of it.

I cannot say I was overjoyed with the finished product. He had struggled like a titan against many frustrating difficulties, paper shortages, lack of staff in the printer's works, and many other most thwarting obstacles. To cap all the printer in charge of the work died during an air raid, and the book was run through the press with my sheaf of corrections omitted.

However, to my joy the book was out.[1]

In January 1943 it was found that Pippa must have another operation. She decided to have it at a nursing home near us.

A few days before she was due to travel she telephoned me, 'Clarice, listen to this!'

She read over the telephone a letter couched in Elizabethan English. Then she explained that she had fallen asleep in the afternoon and when she awoke this letter was found written on the writing pad which lay beside her.

Before she left home two more letters were written in the same style through her hand.

After her operation, which proved to be pretty serious, I visited her daily. For a while she was very weak and in pain and she had a cough which tore her. Indeed we were all very anxious. But strange to say this made no difference at all to the ability of our Teacher to use her. Whereas her own speech was faint and low and breathless, his was as resonant and forceful as ever.

I was startled when first he appeared. She was lying in her private room in the nursing home and I was sitting by the gas fire trying as usual to give out healing power towards her. She was supposed to be sleeping.

Suddenly he was there. The sign of the Cross was given and his powerful soul burned through her wan face.

I was alarmed, for nurses were likely to burst in at any moment.

He said, 'I must not keep this child long. She is weak still. You have helped her a great deal. She was very nearly out this time. Quite a bit of shouldering and pushing was necessary to keep her in the body. You see, it is not yet realized on this plane the strain that two such operations within two years constitute, and the extent and depth of the shock to the entity, as you will of course understand. But she is doing well now.'

He stayed only a few minutes, but I was immensely relieved by his coming, especially as Pippa always felt strengthened and exhilarated by the healing effect he was able to infuse into her.

[1] *The Wisdom of the Spirit* is now in revised form.

A few days later Pippa was sitting up in bed and feeling stronger. To my astonishment she began to write. Letters simply poured from her pen – Elizabethan letters, purporting to come from a wife in her country manor, amongst her family and friends, to her husband from whom she was often separated while he was at Court. In Pippa's exceedingly weak condition one would not have thought she could have held a pen. But the pen flew over the pages, the letters streamed through and we took the greatest delight in their spontaneous charm and rich archaic English. These were to throw light on one of my past lives.

Thus, in spite of war and the disastrous news that filled the newspapers and poured to us over the wireless at that time, our spirits were high.

With Mr Churchill we treasured the thought that 'the springs of our offensive are slowly compressing'.

Pippa came back to our house to recuperate. Needless to say, she spent a good deal of time either in bed or resting, and still she wrote. Forty or so letters in colourful Tudor style streamed from her pen. She avowed that they were nothing to do with her and she did not know whence they came.

'A little exercise to teach something,' whispered the inner voice to me.

Gradually Pippa regained strength, and soon it would be time for her to return home. Very occasionally our Teacher had come to speak with us, but with increasing rareness.

Once I asked him, 'When you speak through Pippa is it as though Pippa's brain is like a typewriter, and you are limited by the number of keys of the typewriter?'

'Not exactly,' he answered, 'but while using a ground-level register it is naturally impossible to convey meanings that can be achieved only in an elevated condition of thought. That should be obvious. This method of speech is simply to give you steerage-way, as it were, to charter the course.'

'But sometimes,' I objected, 'in the Silence you drop something so enigmatical into my mind. I take it and wander into the woods of thought, and wonder and wonder if I have you aright.'

'And what pride and joy I take in watching you wander in the woods – working things out for yourself. Search only for wisdom. And find rest too, in the Silence. Draw from the Source of all things power and wisdom, that Source which you know so well how to tap. And try not to fly with wings but half-fledged.'

'But will you not explain to me – like this – more exactly what this is all about, where we are heading for?'

'We are heading for perfection. But that is still a long way off.' And he leaned forwards and spoke with sudden fervour. 'It is so mighty a thing, so tremendously important. I trust you understand me?'

I was silent. I wondered if I did understand him.

Then I burst out childishly, 'But with everything so ordinary and real and solid around me, it is so difficult to realize.' I was often so desperately anxious that I was failing some plan for me but half understood.

'You are now living in this world. The things around you are real. You must keep your two worlds separate, and keep your feet well planted upon the earth. There is so much love around you. Love is around thee everywhere. Be happy! Do not worry. Come, smile!'

And later to some query of mine he answered, 'That is a thing which you can work out for yourself. We have thrown away the spoon!'

This time of wonder was hard to bear with equanamity. Either I was exalted and joyous, or in the depths of perplexity. In vain did I struggle for that balance of mind that I knew our Mentor needed of me. Always I was struggling with my own expanded consciousness and the wonders that it opened to me, or trying to polish the receiving instrument of my mind so as to perfect my control, so as to come into close intunement with the Planes above. I found it difficult and painful to switch my mind, my entire personality, from the striving of the inner way, sharply to the cheerful atmosphere of my family. By 4.30 in the afternoon my inner adventuring must be laid aside for some hours, for my boy would return from school, and soon my husband would be home from his office.

Of course this juxtaposition of atmosphere was a safety valve, and I realized that it was excellent in its stabilizing effect. I used to try to do as I was instructed and keep my two worlds separate; but the magnetic pull towards the celestial Mountains tore at me always.

PROGRESS AND PUBLICATION

Each evening we made music. We were a trio of piano, flute and violin, and we played gramophone records too of Bach, Mozart, Beethoven, Handel, César Franck and others to delight us. We ignored the air raid warnings that continually droned in the distance, and the music drowned the thrum of the German bombers on their nightly path overhead to Bristol or other towns in the North and West. Exeter was flattened in her centre, and we did not expect another such visitation.

One night before Pippa was completely restored to health, Wystan was doing his 'fire-watching' duty in the city (which involved standing upon the roof of his office building awaiting a rain of incendiary bombs). My son was safely tucked up in bed.

Pippa and I settled ourselves for an evening's music.

Our celestial Mentor suddenly appeared.

'I would talk with thee for a few minutes about the cord,' he said, 'but first of all, there is no reason now why Pippa should not return home the week after next. Now that the cord be finally linked again she will be all right. And there is much for her to do at home. I want to tell you about the cord which links life with what is called "death". The cord is the vibrational link which joins one body to the next. It is like an electric light plug, it insulates the voltage.' And he made a gesture towards the point for the lamp nearby. 'In cases of shock the cord becomes attenuated, stretched; severe shock causes it to break, which of course means that you die. In convalescence the cord gradually mends, becomes strengthened until, as in the case of Pippa, it is completely restored. Do you understand me?'

'Yes,' said I, 'I do, but I don't quite see the technical working of it.' I was fishing for more, as I felt that, as so often was the case, he was speaking of this subject because he wished to make known to me something quite other than the reason for Pippa's growing health. We would fence as swordsmen do, feinting and saying things of little inner significance (compared with our conversations in the Silence or the watches of the night), both knowing there was much that reticence and a curious fastidiousness or discrimination upon mystical subjects which prevented us speaking aloud about them. But I tried to get him to speak more fully upon certain religious problems that did not yet make a clear pattern in my mind. Here perhaps was a chance to draw him out.

'Do you not see,' he went on, 'the reason for the umbilical cord which joins the babe to the mother? The cord of which I speak is much the same in functioning. It is the vibrational link between all the bodies.'

Then he said, 'And I shall have to give you pain.'

'I don't mind the pain,' I said.

'You always had courage.' Then he leaned forward and pressed both thumbs firmly into the centre of my forehead with a lifting movement. Then he said lightly, 'This be nice. But I must to my fire-watching!' (I knew he referred to the fact that the many human beings whom he watched over seemed to him as little 'fires of light'.)

And with the sign of the Cross he was gone.

That was February 1943, and he did not come again in that fashion.

Ten days later Pippa returned home, restored to health.

Our beloved Instructor from the Beyond had not said that he would never speak again through Pippa – but he never did, for thirteen years.

I was now at sea in the open boat of my own mind, and as he had once said, I had to 'use my oars'.

I continued my practices of the Silence, knowing now that there was a guiding Hand on the other side of the curtains of silence, ever ready to assist and direct, school or scold me. It was a privilege beyond all imagining.

One more word as to his method during our inter-telephonic communication between the two worlds. He never used the sort of phraseology that one would expect. Always he expressed himself in colourful and surprising idiom. He used allegory, myth, the most telling metaphor, or even current colloquialisms. I learned immensely from his mere choice of words. Always his answer to a query of mine, rocketed into his dimension, would return couched surprisingly, or with some refreshing turn of phrase or word-usage that illuminated by its 'double entendre'.

He developed the system of using code words. These were words or phrases carefully chosen, whose meaning contained a double sense, or if one put the beat upon another syllable, a different meaning became apparent. He would use omnibus words from which there often could be mined a whole wealth of meaning which cast a brilliant light upon the subject with which

I was struggling. Occasionally in the Silence, he would use a Latin phrase or sentence, a language which I had never learned, with the recommendation to 'memorize this and ask your husband to translate'. When this was done, the translated phrase would contain the answer to my query. All these methods were used by that master-mind in order to demonstrate to me continually that the Voice in the Silence was his very own, and not my imagining. For these curious and sometimes exasperating methods of reply, I am eternally grateful. I say 'exasperating' because often those code words would take weeks to unravel. Indeed some have never been elucidated yet, and it is part of the 'rules of the game' that he should never explain the meaning of a code word. I must seek its inner meaning myself – or else lose what was offered.

His figures of speech illuminated his angle of living. Once he called himself a 'lily farmer'. This graphic phrase taught me how those privileged human beings whom he tended – as well as looking to him like little lights or fires – sometimes looks like glowing flowers, opening and closing to light. Once he held in front of my eyes the most vital and solid-seeming picture of a carpenter's spirit-level, but it was of a radiant gold, and the shape of it was formed out of the letters FIRE. The message it contained was that 'the level of spirit depends upon the balancing of the fire therein'.

Thus, and thus, and thus, in a thousand subtle ways did he educate his willing pupil.

Thus did the Teacher try to polish the reflector of my mind upon the whetstone of his knowing.

For all was not given in words. These were only 'lifebelts' thrown out occasionally to the floundering swimmer who could not make the shore. More often explanation was given in flashes of vision, or in series of experience, in which it seemed as though my mind was wafted out of itself, and taught to function upon a new plane of being.

Here all things looked different.

It seemed as though one had lived all one's life in a walled garden, till suddenly a giant bird had swooped, and taken one out of that enclosure with its high impenetrable walls and carried one up onto the shoulder of some lofty mountain. At last one could see the surrounding countryside, the valleys, the rivers, the streams that fed each river, the mountains and their turrets of snow. And beyond, one could see the ocean which fed the streams with rain, and the sky.

In company with the Instructor from another world I learned continually. A whole philosophy of religion gradually percolated into my mind, drop by drop, which was new to me and which I could share with my husband.

Chapter Fourteen

UNDERSTANDING AND FRUSTRATION

1

My husband and I could not bring ourselves to speak to anyone of these – to the orthodox amongst whom we lived – most unrespectable happenings. Only to two or three intimate friends did we divulge these supernatural occurrences. I dreaded arguments and explanations, and the inevitable exposure of our treasure to the wintry blasts of incredulous attack.

Experience teaches that it is useless to lay before men and women of conventional thought ideas for which their minds are unprepared. They shy as horses do when a bird lifts over a hedge, and if what is new to them does not fit in with their preconceived patterns of thought and belief they rail against it.

So we took the cowardly but safer course of remaining silent.

This may have been our error. On an occasion when our Teacher was talking with us, he said, 'Share the pleasure of your treasure', and it is possible that we should have been wiser to blurt out our story and take the consequences rather than keep 'our treasure' to ourselves. I had no wish to keep all that I was learning to myself. Indeed, when one thinks that one has found an elixir of living, one yearns to give it out to all who will listen. But I was diffident of seeming 'too big for my boots'. So I published my first book, *The Wisdom of the Spirit*, under an assumed name, 'Armido'. Only a handful of friends knew that I had written it.

I sent the book to an old friend whom I had not seen for some years, without disclosing the authorship. Her reaction was typical of many, 'This would be so wonderful if it were true, but upon what authority does the author speak?'

And so began for me a time of frustration and much difficulty. I felt like a high explosive that would not go off – stuffed with the fireworks of the Spirit, yet unable to give it out. For had not our celestial Visitor declared that to write books had been his own idea, and that I was to fit myself to give out what I had been given? But looking around me in those days I could not find any who might be sympathetic seekers upon the same path. I lived among orthodox Church of England folk (my father-in-law was a vicar), and the tide of general doubt and criticism was still dammed up by a conservatism which was not to break out till some twenty years later. My husband and I felt that we had received an illumination of so much that had been puzzling before, yet we were unable to find a way to share with those who were perplexed as we ourselves had been, that which we had found. We felt we now had a yardstick upon which to measure the basic values of life, which gave the first glimmerings of a spiritual Order which rendered wisdom and mercy out of chaos, law out of apparent dissonance.

Cause and effect were seen to be the links in the chain of events which showed all to be the sure working of a law, in spiritual matters as well as physical, the one within and counterpart of the other. This especially in those events wherein we were used to think of God the Father as director.

Was not our world suffering as it had never suffered before? Did not the cry go up on all sides: Why does God allow these things to happen?

And we found that all that happens in this world is the just effect of earlier causes; we ourselves were responsible.

The first Law of the Divine Order was the Law of Light. If we fill ourselves with Light which is Love, and give this out always, only good can come. Light and Darkness became the slide-rule of values. Just as light dispels darkness upon the physical plane, so does the working of the Law of Love dispel evil. Nothing else matters.

The Scale of Reality was seen to rise from the slow, frigid, dark energies of rock and dense matter, up to the incandescent energies of heat and light . . . and so on upwards as the Scale spirals into ever subtler vibrations of Infinity. Each group of octaves of energy – made of the Rays – spreads itself out laterally, creating a universe, a world such as we live in. The one below, unknown to us, is darker and denser, the one above more filled with light, normally unknown to us too. We are limited in our perceptions by our capacity to tune in with finer vibrations. The path of man is to fit himself for living in the upper altitudes by taking into himself more of the Light supernal. This is the basis of all religion. All dogmas, all precepts have at their root the single purpose, to teach and help men to rise. All religions seek to show us how to conquer the downward drag of Earth. Our bodies answer the gravitational pull of the rocky masses of Earth, our spirits, woven as they are of the inner dimensions of Light, answer the upward call of that Spiritual Fire. It is as simple as that.

I saw that where there is more Light there is more God, subtler qualities of mind, richer powers of spirit, more love.

From the base of our universal order, the dense rocks, up through the layers of the oceans, vegetation, animal life, human life and on into the realms of Spirit, the controlling factor is speed of activity of the energies of which each layer is made. With greater frequency of energy there is more warmth, greater light, richer complexity of the divine energies, all being built from the outflowing Rays of the Divine Mind. The qualities, the potentialities of Divine Mind are in all things, but in a rising scale of degree. . . . Less in rock, more in vegetation, and so on up the scale of development in nature. The units of mind which form the inner spirals of the atom, when united in greater complexity, make the cell of life. And so on up the scale, more complexity of the building bricks of the Universe, which are the Ray-energies given forth from the Most High, show forth as a higher form of life and mind and Spirit.

All that we do, all that we think, causes us to rise or fall upon this great Scale. We are where we are now because of our past habits of thought, our past reactions to experience. We each one of us vacillate continually either up or down this mighty Ladder of Degree.

I learned that this Ladder, this Scale, this Order of Degree, like the atom, turns in a spiral in upon itself, so that in its lower registers the energies fix into physical substances, into the heat and light of fire, of suns and stars. These are the outward dimensions of created things. As the spiral turns in upon itself, the planes or dimensions, made of those inner energies, increase their frequency. They give off light which to human eyes is invisible. And all things which are of that inner dimension are of a frequency, a light, suitable to that condition or framework. With each turn of the spiral inwards the scale of energies increases in frequency, in light, in purity, in power, in holiness. The energies which make that level stretch outwards into a dimension or plane of beings. All things on that plane are constructed of like energies suitable to that plane of existence.

Men and women who leave the body at death live upon those planes which are suited to their Spirit's condition. It is a matter of automatic adjustment. And there are as many invisible planes of human existence in the Within as there are grades of souls on Earth . . . and many higher. The planes progress ever onwards into the Divine Vortex of Infinity.

The Ultimate, the Source of all Light, is the Mind of the Most High. The radiant properties of His Mind stream outwards from the Central Source and fill the Universe, they weave all that is. Therefore the properties of the Mind of the Most High are existent in all things – in accordance with their degree. The Central Source is Light Supernal, all perfection, all holiness, all Mind, all Being, all beatitude, all bliss. THAT, the Inexpressible, is above all qualities that we can name. The Radiations from THAT bring with them the qualitative Powers of Creation.

Thus, to quote the words of the Teacher: 'Every cubic centimetre is shot through with all that is.'

The Ultimate *is* all things.

The world is blind only because it is in its infancy.

What men term 'sin' is not sin as such, but ignorance. It is the inevitable ignorance of children, young and inexperienced upon the path of evolution. In the realms of nature all are learning but only man begins to see. Intelligence and awareness dawn, and he begins to look up and penetrate the essence of life and being which exists as Cause behind all manifestation, the Most High.

All that we are and think and create and do exists for ever about this planet as a complex weave of energy-charges, a dynamic cloak worn by Earth, pregnant of its past, redolent of its future. The quality of this aura draws to it the clouds and sunshine of future events. Each unit of life, each ego is vitally important for this reason. Each one contributes to the magnetic action of the whole, causing the future conditions of life on Earth. Each one is responsible for the planet's well being.

I came to realize the reason for the gulf between two types of human being, those with a tendency towards faith or intuitive

UNDERSTANDING AND FRUSTRATION

knowing, and those without. I learned that this has but little to do with education, with intellect or reason, or even mental development. Indeed the highly educated often fall in the latter class, those without intuitive knowing, simply because they distrust their own inner faculty. A natural and often unconscious contact with a level of the inner dimensions of being creates the channel of acceptance. Those who focus powerfully through their brains, using primarily the mental levels, sometimes tend to shut themselves off from the spiritual registers. More often, those who are ill-equipped with powers of intellect, country folk or the primitive races, achieve intuitive contact with the invisible dimensions, albeit not necessarily the elevated levels. They accept intunement unquestioningly as a child would, uninhibited by intellectual doubts.

With the intellect we can but perceive and analyse; with the heart we know. For a proper understanding both are needed, held in balance.

Contact with the inner levels can be made easier and more acutely conscious by the practice of meditation and mental discipline, but even then a sharp watch is needed to steer the ego clear of levels of thought or being which are emotional or 'negative' and debased. Like tunes in with like. According to the wavelength set up in the mind is intunement brought about with like levels. This is the value of using the old religious terms to lift and purify the mind before meditation is embarked upon. A line or verse of a psalm or prayer carries with it, if used with intent, the wavelength achieved in elevated states by the poet, and so by repeating it one takes on the vibration of intunement with a higher register of spiritual being. One is carried up. True seekers need honesty of purpose, a clear analytical mind, and a selfless design of giving all they have gathered in. Compassion purifies and heats the mind and thrusts it upwards.

The intellectual man or woman tends to focus so strongly in the mental registers that the channels are insulated away from the levels whence intuition comes. This is why scientists and academicians of this type tend to cut themselves off from the dimensions of spiritual knowing. A sort of pack ice sets about the mind so that they are unable to feel the grace whence the fire of spiritual knowing flows. They confine their brains within the limits of empiric and logical reasoning, saying that they can find no evidence for the power of the Spirit. They little realize that they have insulated themselves from the well-spring of fire within which is the very truth they seek.

In meditation the aspirant is able to penetrate deeper and assimilate more completely what is perceived, and concepts studied take on the atmosphere of experience rather than study. Thus the new understanding gained becomes a part of the inner being.

Contact with the spiritual realms within, which is so easy for some, can be learned by all. It is the prime medicine for the soul. It pleases, comforts, helps, soothes, rests and sustains, as well as elevating and giving enlightenment to those who seek. It gives a sense of drawing upon a power and grace greater than one's own. It feeds and builds up, it expands the soul and increases the powers of mind, memory and character. It gives the light of hope and courage to all.

It is the cutting off of this channel of Divine Grace which is endangering our race today. This is not a matter of following one religion, one sect more than another, for all teach the same truth in one form or another. Scepticism, doubt and downright disbelief, engendered by the rigid usage of the scientific attitude, and the falling away from religious trust, is starving the human race of its natural birthright, the sunshine of the Spirit which alone feeds and sustains the soul. It is there, ever-offered as the sun's rays are offered, but we cannot make it ours unless we open the windows of the mind and soul to let it in.

Lack of this practice, whether conscious or unconscious, is causing the nerves of the civilized races to crack under the strain of modern living. All the medical treatment in the world cannot supply what one breath of the Spirit can give in soul-sustenance, peace and hope.

Chapter Fifteen

LIGHT AND DARKNESS

1

The methods of teaching were many and varied.

Sometimes I was taken to places of breath-taking beauty. Once, when in the Silence, I found myself suddenly in a realm so exquisite that it was hard afterwards to adjust oneself to earth's shadowy condition. Words dry up as means of description.

I was in a world where coloured fire formed the texture of things. There was the seeming of an enclosed space with walls and objects such as one might expect in a palace; but where walls should have been a gauze of shell pink hung and quivered like an aurora and those objects which were around were iridescent fires, luminous with colours unknown on earth.

They radiated gold, turquoise, peach, but were so much more than this, for each had a fire which gave it a life of its own. Within each thing was a light which moved within itself as little secret flames.

The glory of the place was a very ecstasy. As I roamed through that heavenly place I found that movement was effortless and feather-light.

Seeming to understand the laws which governed this condition I determined to add to what I found there. I would make, with thought, some sheaves of flowers to hang upon the shining walls. And so, with an effort of mental will, I called into being festoons of flowers to deck the place. But though I thought of them as flowers they appeared as something quite other. They were fairy things, living and vibrant, of rainbow light, fire-filled and gleaming. Each sheaf shone with a light and joy which was the essence of its being, each radiating outwards its own beaming potence.

Thus did I learn that Fire is the very essence of all that is, Fire which has the properties of Mind.

It was explained to me then – though words were not used – that this was the stuff of the Rays. The Rays were essences divine, given forth by the Mind and Being of the Most High. All things in heaven and earth were woven of this glory. According to their place on the Ladder of Degree they formed things which were light-filled and gossamer as here in these elevated planes, or things that were dense and dull, fixed and cold. This was the difference between heaven and earth: light and heat, or darkness and cold. All planes of living find their place between these two extremes. And the Divine Rays were the substance of all creation. They held within them the essence of light and love and mind. They were beamed forth from the Supreme Source, radiations from the Mind of the Most High, carrying with them the qualities of His thought. All things in all worlds were weavings of these radiant energies; woven together in varying proportions they created everything that is.

I learned that the Rays are the stuff of what men call angels. The human forms of angels are, of course, the imaginings of human kind, or sometimes implanted into the human mind for a divine purpose.

Angels are 'extensions of consciousness' emanating from the creative action of the Mind and Being of the Most High, implementing His design.

They are the Ray-angels, named in the holy writings and designated by the inspired artists of old in their own colours. The Red Angel, the Blue Angel, the Gold....

The creative Rays are therefore of angelic stuff, and all things are made of them in like proportion as they have come together in evolution through the divine law of attraction or love.

Thus is the littlest flower of the stuff of angels.

Rocks and crystals, vegetation, flowers and trees, all organic life, our bodies and our inner selves are woven of selections of these angelic Rays. And because each and every spark of energy which is of the Rays is a unit of mind, there is therefore mind in everything. A unit of mind lies within the vortex of every atom.

Each atom vibrates into the infinity of the Mind of God.

Hence all things are based in Him.

Complexity of these exquisite Ray-elements makes the life and consciousness in organic things. I saw that the greater the variety of these Ray-essences compounded into a living form, the more advanced are the properties of life and mind in it.

These sublime Rays are naturally down-graded as they flow

towards Earth and living things grow upon certain of the outer as well as the refining inner levels of them. Upon their subtlest frequencies are our Spirits made.

Words from my Teacher sounded in my ear: 'The simplicity of design in a blade of grass is the measure of its ignorance.'

Thus is life explained.

All is made of God, of the effluences of His Mind and creative out-giving.

Thus was shown me the reality of those early words of the Teacher: 'There is mind within mind within mind vibrating into infinity.' For I could see that God Himself lay at the heart of all things. It is for us to strive to enrich ourselves upon an ever greater inflow of His Divine Rays.

2

It was by reason of experiences such as these that I began to understand a fraction of the Laws of Creation. I learned what all the reading in the world could not teach me, for experience itself becomes a part of one's inner knowing.

I was in meditation once when suddenly it seemed as though the whole sky of my mind opened and I saw a vision of splendour. It was as if the whole area of Devon where we lived was viewed from a high hill and below I could see the city in the valley with the shining estuary beyond. Then the whole sky was filled with a flaming Being which took upon itself the form of a sunflower, luminous and fiery. The Being presided, as it were, over the hills and valleys. It was in its essence of angelic stuff, like burnished copper, and all the landscape shone with the reflected Light.

I knew that this was not reality but a form designed to explain to me the expanded state of a Being no longer human.

'I am like a sheet of lightning about the Earth,' my Teacher once said to me. And this vision was created to suggest to me the condition of living of an expanded Spirit of great power.

Shortly after this an artist of genius, of inspiration, a friend who lived far away, altered his style of painting, turning to abstract designs. Picture my astonishment when, some months after these experiences just described (of which, of course, I had spoken to no one), he came to see us and gave me several of his new works. Two were peach-coloured fantasies in pastels, representing the flowers which I had created mentally in spiritual form in the heavenly place which I had visited. The third was the golden, sunflower-shaped Being who had filled the sky of my vision.

And now, fifteen years later, we live on those hills depicted in the vision and in the picture, over which the Presence presided.

I know that these sound like fantastic imaginings. Yet if I do not give what I have been given I break the law – for these things were shown to demonstrate the Power, the ubiquity of the Spirit and the way it works.

3

On another occasion a very different experience came to me, one of stark and gloomy horror.

'You remember well the scale of the Rays,' said my Teacher one day – in the inner Planes of the Silence. 'Learn them from the lower end of the Ladder of Degree. Come and see the lower end of the scale.'

Soon I found myself in an underground cavern. The air was heavy as ice and dark, and there was a sense of unbearable gloom and terror in all I saw. Standing around these endless caves were monoliths, lumps of rock and stone of all sizes and shapes. But I knew that these ghastly rocky creatures were the relics of life. Such a sense of horror gripped me that had not my Mentor stood beside me I should have instantly operated the mental lift of light within me and fled the place.

These creatures were unable to move. They had become still and cold and fossilized. The energies in them and of which they were made were gradually slowing down and ceasing all activity. The pillars of stone had limbs most curiously made like fungus or in the bizarre shapes of some cactus, or like the great woody growths one sees upon the trunk of an old oak tree. Some had heads that looked like this too. There were forests of them. All along the caverns were these terrible creatures fettered by their own innate lack of the life-giving energies of fire into a state of fossilization to the spot where they stood. And from all of them came an emanation of icy pitiless malice, which is indescribable. I felt that cold hatred for one another in their one-time hearts had brought them to this metallic state of petrification.

There in the gloom and the solitude they were doomed to

await the steadily increasing desiccation of their one-time quickened lives.

I remembered Lot's wife who 'looked back' towards evil and was turned into a pillar of salt.

And I knew now why that allegory had been given and why this was shown to me. It was to point the parallel between the light and dark, good and evil, love and hate, fire-energy and solid ice. These creatures now fossilized were doomed to await a renewal of life in a new world order, when they would be fragmented into elements and given the chance to build themselves anew.

I wondered how the concept of hell as a place of fire had crept into the human imagination. For this I knew was the ultimate perdition.

Perdition came from losing altitude, losing heat, losing light, losing love, losing the vibrant faculties of the Divine Mind which are ever offered in the Rays which shower through the whole Cosmos and which are drawn into us through thought.

If we refuse to think with warmth and loving kindness we slip back upon the Path of Development.

This was the next key to the puzzle. I worked to make a logical pattern of this living Universe.

'How do we grow?' I asked in the Silence. 'Why do some draw to them faculties of light and love, while others gradually drop back and ossify? How does it come about – in justice and mercy?'

'I have already made this known to you. Magnetic thought is the way.'

The answers came to me sometimes in words, but more often in thought-forms which I must strive to render in words.

'I give you my vision, you must clothe it in words,' said my Mentor inwardly.

Magnetic thought – like attracts like. The pieces fell into position.

Thought being magnetic energy draws to itself other Ray-energies in affinity with the thought sent out. So that thinking man is building into himself more energies like to his own thoughts. Man is sculpturing himself as he thinks and acts.

'Then what about evolution? What about the Darwin theory? How do animals and man arrive at their present condition?'

These thoughts thrummed through my mind.

Answer was never given me gratis. Always I was made to work for it. Always I had to shape the problem, think all round it, and struggle to fit it to the pattern of things as they are. Thus I found that understanding gained through meditation was more penetrating and became more clearly defined and a part of one, than by study.

'The magnetism of the power of thought is the magic behind all evolution,' said the Voice within. 'The little creature washed up by the tide and left gasping on the hot sands needed lungs, it needed legs to carry it toward the cool shade of the trees. It gasped, it struggled, it longed for the means of breathing and locomotion. Desire was the mainspring of its growth.'

'Yes, but it died. It died before it got its lungs and legs.'

'True, but you forget that other factor, renewal. Death is not real. It is in appearance only. The creature that died on the shore merely sloughed off its insufficient garment, its body without legs or lungs. Woven of the inner Rays of Spirit, it was not harmed. Most vital of all, its efforts to breathe and to move had activated the law of magnetic attraction: it strove to breathe, it drew into itself the first elements of the faculties which in time would make lungs. These were not lost through death, only the body was lost. The Ray-ingredients drawn to it by gasping efforts were woven indelibly into its inner levels of being. Soon it would be renewed, born again into a physical body carrying within it those rudimentary units of energy which over years – and lives – of effort, would make the breathing apparatus that it so urgently desired. The same process gave it legs. Each flap of its fins, each struggle up the shore, strengthened its limbs. Scientists on earth tell you that usage of a limb strengthens and increases it, but they neglect to tell you why.

'In evolution, need and desire are magnetic influences, and the prime operators of the creative principle.'

'Then God does not create each creature as it is – and man too?'

'Each creature has created itself over the ages. The principle of renewal – the unbroken continuity of the individual spirit whether in physical living or in the planes beyond – is the ground of all evolution. It provides the ground for growth throughout the whole of nature. The creature – or the human being – dies, withdraws into the next planes, carrying with him the blue-print

LIGHT AND DARKNESS

of his "Ray-energy content", his divine qualities. When he returns – or is born again after a period for rest and consolidation – he returns once more bearing with him the same Ray-essences which he has drawn into himself up to the present. These are reflected in the physical genes and chromosomes. The faculties which he develops, be he animal or man, depend entirely upon this blueprint.'

'But doesn't he take from his parents all sorts of qualities which are not really like his own?'

'You are born of parents who are suited to your Ray-content. This is an axiom. This means that a creature is born to the type of animal whose overall equation, or energy-content, approximates to his own. Those gains which he made last time, in his struggle up the hot beaches, for instance, will show in what the biologists call a mutation. He will produce just that fragment more of a certain type of energy which will help him next time in his battle for life on the sandy shore. Darwin was right that this mutation gives him an increased survival value, but he did not realize that the method of transmitting that mutation was the continuity of living – over the bridge called "death". Each little creature collected its own mutations through effort, through passionate need to survive, through intense activity of a specific kind, and carried those new energy gains with him through the portals of death, over into the Beyond. Later these were reflected back again into his fresh body on earth. They show as genes, chromosomes and other factors in the physical make-up.'

'And in man too these same laws operate?'

'Most certainly. They operate with even greater force, because the mind of man is more powerful, more concentrated than in an animal. The mental habits of a man, no matter how subconscious, or how unaware he is of them, draw to him by the Law of Magnetic Attraction precisely those Ray-energies which are like to the thoughts sent out.

'He is forging himself, in all his levels of being through the thoughts of his heart and spirit, out of the energies which are drawn to him by his habits of thought.

'I told you earlier that a man only inherits physical things from his parents, the soul and spirit of a man are his own, he has evolved them himself by his reactions to experience over the past ages.

'Thus does the All-Wise Parent give free rein to the creative action within every one of His creatures. When a man fails, it is no one's fault but his own. When a man shines with the inner light of the Spirit he does so because he has used his own effort to fill himself with the light of God.'

'But does not God help His creatures? Does not His grace give them succour?'

'The world must be maintained by Laws and not by the arbitrary intervention of the Most High. Where would be the honour and glory in a triumphing Spirit if he were merely the puppet of a dictator God? Yet His Grace is of course the strength and saving glory of each and every one of us. But it is always offered, not fitfully, capriciously. The Rays, with all their spiritual benefits, cascade towards us always.

'It is for man to learn how to conduct them to him. When this becomes a part of his conscious way then he begins to climb aloft more swiftly.'

Chapter Sixteen

CHRONICLES OF FIRE

1

My long habit of diary writing produced a chronicle not of outward events, but of experience, conversations and discoveries in the inner worlds of Spirit.

My journal acted as a focal point for these adventures of the mind. Within its pages I could record exactly as they had taken place and as truthfully as fumbling words could describe, those discoveries which were milestones upon the way to understanding. It was somehow comforting to lay out in wholesome words on paper events which certainly I would have forgotten had I not recorded them instantly.

This practice steadied my nerves. I addressed my journal to my Teacher in the Beyond, and everything was laid before his invisible eyes as a record of my periods of study. And so this hour or so of writing each morning became in itself a useful exercise.

Since there are nearly a hundred of these books filled with my jottings over the past twenty-five years, I will quote only a few extracts chosen at random – for I have not read them through since.

September 4, 1943
'A new type of consciousness has begun to take hold of me. I can only describe it by an analogy. It is as though my mind expands into a further dimension – Before, I have been as a kettle filled with warm water, localized and heavy, but now the kettle is on the boil and my mind's essences extend beyond me like steam pouring out of the spout and permeating the air around.

'You say that this is your usual condition of freedom; that thus you are able to live within and behind those you love and teach, with a deep caring for their lives and hopes. You gave me a brief glimpse, almost the actual experience of this expanded state of consciousness, of sharing in the lives of those in whom you are involved through loving contact. It was a dazzling experience and love burned within you. And when I was back in myself again I exclaimed, "What *are* you?"

'"I am nothing," you answered. "These are my fold. They are the chickens under my feathers."

'Sometimes you explain this state of expanded living with other analogies. You describe yourself as being like the captain of a great ship, and those you teach are the passengers and crew with whom you are in constant contact. You whispered, "The flight deck holds in tender convoy the core of English hearts."

'Yet this does not mean that your interest is only among the English, for often you quote activities in other lands.'

Then I find an entry: 'At night-time it is difficult to sleep because of the light in my head. You told me to focus upon black velvet – in imagination – so as to douse down the image of the light within – and so to help me to sleep.'

This brings to mind the subject of visualization, for I was trained upon the magic of this power in the human mind.

I was taught that to imagine a wavelength, a pattern of thought, is to create it. And to create it in one's own head is to tune in with that wavelength in the great Beyond. Thus the holding of the concept of Divine Light or Holiness, to focus on this thought, to love it, to crave it, inevitably sets up in one the wavelength of acceptance. This is the basis of prayer. This too is the magic behind the Christian message. To imagine, to visualize, to seek to be with and emulate the Beloved Master Jesus, drew the countless members close to Him, to the wavelength of His love and purity, to His Light.

The power of visualization cures and humbles by causing a fusion with a Light beyond one's own.

Yet sometimes in those early years of my endeavour I would range upwards in the Silence with the mind's antennae and find no answering word from my Teacher.

September 7, 1943

'I begged to know why so many hours of silence? My head was filled with Light and I knew your presence, but there was no

instruction, no word. But later you told me that you "were experimenting with the second form of speech".
' "What is that?" I asked.
' "Speaking direct into your mind without words," was the answer.
'I said, "I recognize the feel of this method, but I find it hard to have faith when your thoughts flood my mind without the form of words. I feel it might so easily be my imagination."
' "Your mind is the screen and I the film projector – in this method," you answered.'

Sometimes a state of ecstasy was put upon me that was strangely hard to bear. I quote:

September 8, 1943
'Last night you flooded me once more with the holy blaze of White Fire, so that I could scarcely keep from crying out, or hold on to my consciousness. This strange agony, this ecstasy of bitter electrocuting pain. . . . It seems to dissect and cut and crumble the very soul into nothingness. You forced it into my inner being so that I was transfixed. And all day today my whole body has felt filled with the white light which is half pain, half sweetness and difficult to support while I am amongst people and doing ordinary tasks.

'Later you caused many thoughts and ideas to loom into my mind, but I could not gather the gist of your instruction. I said, "It cannot be said that we are having a very clear conversation."

'But then I realized how little it matters to you that the conversation does not appear to be clear and the train of thought lucid. In fact, if you wished it to be clear, then clear it would be. Gone are the days when I struggled for clarity of communication between us, thinking that it is the failure of my own mind or some foggy atmospherics which keep our thought apart. For now I realize that what I want or desire governs the situation not at all. So long as the "line" is confused I must struggle to clear it and to understand, but this may be an exercise or discipline imposed by you. So it is with all my desires. So it is with my longing for wider vision, so it is when I long for you to talk with me in the old familiar way through Pippa, so that I can hear with my ears and can savour your realness . . . and you don't come any longer thus.

"You must get rid of all desires, all weakness," you said. So the fact that I long for them is reason for your withholding them. Then you showed me a "flash" of a trayful of white cups; any little residue of water must be dried out of each cup. You indicated that these were spiritual centres which must be cleansed and perfected.

' "To reach perfection is agony," you said. "The Wheels of Fire must be balanced and cleansed for one's final release." '

September 19, 1943

'Last night I had put much effort into prayer. We had been discussing the whole race of man and I said to you how saddened and worried I felt to see how recalcitrant, how "wet and cold" and lowly we all are.

' "Why?" you asked point blank.

'That "Why" startled me. Why was I worried and saddened? It set me thinking. And then I saw that this was nothing to fret about since we are all on the Path of Development, which is like a moving staircase up which, if we will it, we are bound to rise. Then I returned in silence to my prayer. I strove to reach the highest Light possible for me. I tried to lift the "skylight" at the crown of my head. And I strove to flood the world with that Light and blessing for which my feeble frame might act as viaduct. Then I felt a great insurge of power and so terrific was the voltage of Light that seemed to cataract through me that I felt that I had achieved some measure of success.

'Then, quick to make sure that I should not puff myself up with self-approbation, when next I came to you, you said, "You *were* a good girl, weren't you!"

'And puff! went the wind out of my sails!

'With many such gentle chidings do you prick the balloon of any fancied pride! But then, in recompense, later you caught me up to receive the white Fire Blaze. Again and again did it penetrate and flood the inner being with its electrocuting power. So violent was its paining force that I could not take it without crying out and tumbling down the white Hill of Consciousness back into my normal state. I strove to take its final blazing influx without crying out. Only once, then, for a few moments did I manage to hold that bliss of agony without losing hold for very pain. Ecstasy called away my consciousness into spheres of Light.

And I felt that my eyes – my real Eyes – were wide open. Yet I did not see you. Since you have said that "disappointment dissects me", I feel that often you hood me like a falcon and despoil my hopes to "see". But I must be patient.'

September 20, 1943
'You give me a vision.

'I was among a mass of people at night time, upon our hilltop, when suddenly all the sky was lit up with a radiant pearly glow. People gazed in fear and amazement. And then I saw hanging pendant, filling all the scene from earth to sky, an unformed vision of the Christ Being, like an arc of fire from whence the white radiance came. I gazed in wonder. And as I came to myself I saw myself bathed in light, reflection of the glory that I had beheld. Thus do we absorb what we contemplate.

'Words hesitate and dry up on the brink of things beyond description.'

2

My Mentor, when last he had spoken to me through Pippa in the open light of day, had said, 'And I must give you pain.' And later, in the Silence, 'Only intense mental agony opens the way.'

Now it seemed that this programme of giving pain was on. There were still the visions, the joys, the instruction, the hand which confidently led me through the mystifications of thought, but it appeared that these delights had need of antidote – rather as a sculptured figure needs a spine of iron within it to stiffen it against its own weakness.

'It is not wished to give your outward life troubles and difficulties, yet suffer you must,' he said. And so my outer life, the life of our family, proceeded with even tenor and with continual fortune and blessing, but my inner life took a dark turn. Suffering of a mental and spiritual kind was infused into my mind which often caused the ship of my equilibrium to rock dangerously and nearly capsize. For days or weeks I would be in a state of inner torment which he said 'would bleed me white'.

He explained that suffering acts upon the human framework within just as a Turkish Bath acts upon the body. In suffering the soul heats to supernatural registers of spiritual temperature and the impurities flow from one and drop away.

'As air is to dying embers so do the bellows of suffering revive the flagging spirit,' he said.

I took it badly.

Over and over again my Teacher explained that this was why I was suffering; he had to do this to free me. Suffering alone could set me free. I found this hard to realize and remember.

At the same time the blessings were increased. I had realized by this time that the life of the Spirit is not governed merely by the beneficent designs of God the Most High, nor the care and loving attention of Holy Ones and Teachers in the Beyond. It is controlled by inflexible laws as precisely as are events and experiments in the physical laboratory. Those in the Invisible who take an interest in our well-being and progress, however wise, however eager to help, are hampered by the Laws of Degree and of Cause and Effect upon which the spiritual currents flow. Just as an electric light bulb cannot be made to shine unless a sufficient power is directed towards it along clear channels and a bulb will either glow feebly or break if a wrong current be used, so the human mind and Spirit cannot take the Holy Fires unless it be tuned to them.

However eager are the wishes of the aspirant to learn and the Teacher to instruct, no direct contact or teaching can be passed through unless wavelength be tuned to wavelength, like to like.

It was made clear to me that this has been the age-long reason for and value of prayer. It is not to beg an inattentive or obdurate Almighty to hold up His Laws so that their effect may not hurt us or fail to give us that which we desire. It is to tune the mind of him who prays to an at-one-ment with the celestial Glory. Only through this synchronization of the Divine effluence with the human soul can the currents of blessing flow in.

I was taught that, as he put it, 'religion is the science of ballistics'. Prayer is the method whereby the quality of inertia can be conquered. The gravitational pull of the earth tugs at us continually and only effortful will can conquer it. Prayer draws upon higher essences and fills the balloon of the soul with finer energies which cause the soul to cut free from the clutch of earth's inertia.

Hence the perennial need for effort.

I learned that the celestial Teacher was engaged upon the task of helping me to use myself with spiritual effort so that some sort of intunement could take place. And many were the methods which he used in order to bring this about.

I learned early that it was no part of his plan to do the work for me. If I did not understand an event or some ruse to make me think or suffer, then I must wrestle with the occurrence alone.

'We have thrown away the spoon,' he said again. 'I want to help you to use your own thought and judgement. I want to help you to be strong and to stand alone.'

Suffering seemed to hold as vital a part in the programme as my studies in the dimensions of Spirit, and my joys. And I found it excessively hard to hold all these contrary stresses in balance. Outwardly my life was full, gay, surrounded by those I loved and who loved me, and it was often almost impossible not to show upon my face the inner strain which I was going through. Yet I must hide it for those about me could be provided with no explanation at all as to why I might suddenly appear strained, exhausted or sad.

'I want you to keep your two worlds separate,' adjured my Mentor, yet it was not always easy to do this. That which took place in the Within was far more eventful, far more exciting and stirring than any events could be on the surface of living. But of course it constituted an antidote and anchorage that I must cook and clean, as well as companion my husband and son. But the inner struggle took some toll of my physical strength and I find a note in a diary of 1944:

'If our ships could bring us more fruit and nuts I should be able to patch up a slender vegetarian diet, and so gain a little more strength.'

But physical strength was not a necessary adjunct to spiritual advancement and my lack of robustness may have made the instrument less inflexible in the hands of the Teacher.

Yet I cannot have been so very much lacking in normal strength for I find a note in the diary of October 6, 1943:

'One would think to read these diaries that I only sit and meditate, write or type. But I am a very busy wife, and "Mum", cook and general factotum. Often I bicycle into the city, have coffee with Wystan at the Old Coffee House over the Roman well in the Cathedral Close, do the shopping and push a heavily-laden bicycle up the long hill home, before getting the lunch. And most days I run around the hills with the dogs before preparing the mid-day meal.'

The celestial Instructor was himself a focal point in the upper altitudes of Spirit which aided me to pin-point my intuitive faculty to a particular wavelength. Through my ever-listening ear I could leap up to his Voice and take hold of the vibration upon which he worked. And when the Voice was not being used, then the Light above could be held by the thrusting of the focus of the mind through the orifice in the crown of the head. It was as if I saw an ever-ascending pathway of Divinity reaching through him, through the Christ of God, up towards the Central Source of Light.

'I am the gateway,' once the Teacher said to me, and as he spoke into the Silence he gave a flashed vision of an archway leading into a great cathedral filled with Light.

And so words, symbols, visions and dreams as well as closely reasoned instruction were given in an attempt to expand my mind gradually towards a deeper understanding of things as they are.

October 14, 1943

'And now I must try to recall and write of the strange blending of suffering and exaltation through which I lived last night. As I sit here writing a letter to Thee in broad sunlight it seems difficult to connect myself with that thing I was.

' "Close your eyes and live it again," you murmur. And this I will do.

'I spent last evening listening to Beethoven's Missa Solemnis. Wystan was out fire-watching. And by virtue of the effort put out during that hour and a half I came up closer to your level than has been possible with my wretchedly fluctuating mind in the last few days. Always such effort is repaid. And as I came so close to your mind it became plain that I must be laid upon a burning altar of sacrifice and in that burning would dissolve the last of "me". My utter dissolving is what you need. And coupled with this need in me for personal destruction was a strangely agonizing thirst for the Fire of the Holy Spirit. I was as one burning in a desert whose soul cries out for water. With all my will I strained up towards that Christ-shower of Light; to drink and to be dissolved, those two wishes were in all the spaces of my consciousness, more vital than life itself. To die, to have the suffering heart burned with the holy blaze and to be dissolved in the power of the Most High . . . to drink, to fill the core of "me" with draughts of the biting crystal fire of the Christ Light.

'I called to you that I suffered.

'And above me I saw a thin fine falling rain of Fire.

'Eagerly I drank. It swelled to a cataract. Thirstily I sought to fill the lightwheel of me with all of It . . . with all its fiery agony. And into the depths of me it drove its exquisite flame-like pain, vivifying me with a thousand needle-points of agony. I seemed to dissolve in Light. Was joy or agony the flame that was me, and yet not me?

'At last I let go. I could bear and support conscious knowing no longer. I cried to you to extinguish me. I remembered your words, "Sleep is a renunciation," and I cried to you to put me to sleep. I thought the pain in my heart would kill me . . . I thought my mind would burst.'

3

October 16:

'You spoke of our efforts to synchronize with the Cosmic Plan. How can I recapture the sense, the essence of all you taught me? I will note down a vision you showed me describing the lives of men in their true proportion. It was thus: The soul of man is an endless crescendo of expanding forces, to be visualized as an unbroken beam of light – to be seen as a coil. His lives as they appear in the body are events which side-step off that growing beam. During each life on earth he goes through experiences which give him opportunity to enrich and cleanse himself upon the Divine Rays. And even during each period of living in the body, one third is spent withdrawn in sleep, for refreshment in lighter atmospheres. Memory and conscious awareness are confined to the waking periods of life, for the purpose of continuity of effort, so as to learn to live the Now. Man is like a spiritual salmon who swims up the Rivers of Life, fighting to get above the weirs into the heavenly places, sometimes wounding himself grievously in the doing. He achieves the glassy pools of the upper reaches, enjoys his period of holiday and refreshment for a long or short time, according to his need and then returns again to the oceans renewed for a fresh period of schooling – with his memory unburdened by his past misfortunes. And once more he starts his battles with the weirs upon the River of Life.

'I saw the spiral development of the individual consciousness, the immense upward urge towards light and love . . . obedience to the call of the Divine. And at last, as each soul triumphs it mingles after centuries of effort with the Being of the Christos. The sacrifice of the Self which is the true joy of Divinity blends each Spirit with the Divine. In this state of expansion of being, each one lays himself out behind and within the conscious living of others in his soul-group of our Cosmic System. This is the reward for triumphant men.

'Finally the Christ Being, the Divine Aspect of the Solar Logos, in loving sacrifice lays down Itself (or Himself), the stuff of the next "World Order". This in the convolutions of Time will produce a yet higher Glory of which we shall be part.

'I saw that we had come – I mean the stuff, the energies of which we here on earth originally were made, had come from earlier and more primeval "world orders" which must have been of far denser material.

'So it is that all life is tending to lift the energies of which it is made into higher states of excellence, drawing ever on those powers which have gone on ahead until a state of Godhood is reached . . . when comes the supreme relinquishment of selfhood. When the God of our System has drawn into Himself all the life which has been raising itself towards Him, then do the physical forms of the stars disappear from the physical Universe, and the warp and woof of a new System is born upon a loftier plane of "World-Order", laid out and formed upon the substances of the Body of the supreme Deity of that System. And so the mighty pattern of evolution starts all over again . . . and thus it has been from earliest "chaos". But there it will commence upon a far finer register, a far higher and more perfect plane than ever before. So are there endless cycles of evolving Deific Systems of Whose Bodies we are diminutive parts. And They, the Celestial Ones, are parts in the Being of the Most High, the Uniplete, the One Supreme. Thus stars appear in our physical sky, live out their age-long lives, wax to their peak as human bodies do. It is the time-span of their chance to gain in that period of existence. Then they decline, melt and disappear to physical eyes and with all their component parts or lives still held into one Whole, They start again their conquering of Wisdom in the task of reforming another body, far more subtle and splendid than the last, another System or Island Universe upon more rarefied essences, of more diverse and radiant divine qualities, of greater perfection and purity, of greater love and light.

'Each new glorified System thus contains the heavenly Spheres of the previous System in its locality in the Space-globe within Its Being.

'This is proceeding now.

'In finer and ever finer conditions do the Almighty Gods process in order serviceable towards a goal of . . . what? A White Fire. . . . A Unity of Divinity in diversity within the single Being of the Most High.

'Thus will ever loftier Universes be made for ever and ever. This is the Vision.'

Chapter Seventeen

DREAMS AND SYMBOLS

1

Much of the teaching was given to me in the form of dreams. When as a girl I had read Freud, Jung and the like, I had learned the attitude to dreams of these pioneers into human thought. But I also made discoveries of my own.

My Teacher in the Invisible used a language of symbolism which was entirely individual. I learned it as we went along, much as one might learn Esperanto. A type of dream would be given me which was as different from the ordinary confused nonsense as chalk from cheese. Indeed one of the code symbols for the power of the Spirit was 'cheese'. I was shown in vision-form curtains of luminous creamy potencies which he called 'milk' or 'cream' or 'cheese' in accordance with the concentration of power which he was describing. This was sometimes used to denote effluences of the Divine, as it downgraded itself towards men on Earth. It was the grace which we could use as Divine food.

Both in dreams and in speech he used words as a new language. For instance *Louis Quatorze* means *Le Roi Soleil* – the Cosmic Lord.

Thus a word could be spoken into my ear, which I must think upon. Sometimes, at last, a symbolic meaning would stand revealed.

He might say of a teacher, 'Yes, he is a Scot.' This puzzled me for a while, knowing that nationality plays no part in these deliberations. Then I realized that a Scot is 'one who comes from the High-lands', or the planes Above.

A T was used to signify self-sacrifice, 'not my will but Thine'. The T indicates the arms outstretched in giving, without the head, the seat of the personal will.

An infinity of subtle meanings were conveyed by this means in a manner which was quite beyond me to invent. The method was used to circumvent the machinations of the subconscious, for often it took a long time for me to unravel the message given me by this tortuous method. Indeed there are some which have never been elucidated yet, for as I have said, it was one of the rules of this game that the Teacher must never translate the code words for me. I must unravel the meaning myself, or else waste the effort used to teach me through that message.

The symbolism was unorthodox to say the least of it. Information was given through the using of concepts, objects or people, places and things in accordance with their particular association for me.

A person whom I knew would be used in a dream or vision, as enacting a certain part, which caused inevitable reactions. I then must figure out what were this person's peculiarities, what did he stand for to me? Perhaps it might be royal power, as in a king, or power-lust as in Mussolini, or a central figure in the Church would stand for ecclesiastical piety, a child for humility and so on. Infinite were the means my Mentor used to explain and demonstrate to me the Laws of Living, the way things happen.

A message or teaching would be passed through to me by use of the word 'soap'. Soap is used for cleaning, therefore a particular uncomfortable experience would be explained as having come to me 'as soap', that is as a cleansing experience. A Turkish Bath drips the person clean. This was used as a symbol too, for the same process. Often he would sum up the lesson to be learned with a succinct phrase, dropped whole, as a crystal into my mind.

I copy from my note books some of the aphorisms which he poured into my mind in the Silence: One such was 'Disappointment or humiliation are the Turkish Bath in which the soul drips clean'.

Air, fire and light were used continually as symbols of the Divine.

'To believe is to come to the fringe . . . for then one feels the impact, the Through-shine of That Which is.'

Such sentences would be slotted into my mind as a colour slide is slotted into a viewer. I would hear it, read it off the screen of my mind, and rush to write it down on the nearest piece of paper to hand, for fear of forgetting it. Often these ideas were given me while I was about the duties of the day, or out shopping, or walking over the hills with my dogs. Sometimes I carried paper and pencil with me to capture these lessons from the Spirit.

Once when I was caressing our beloved golden Labrador the Teacher spoke into my mind with dry humour, 'In my day dogs were kept for sport and not for worship!'

He used the symbol of the potato to illustrate his own ubiquity. A potato has many 'eyes', all belonging to the one white body. 'My eyes are everywhere. Where I love there am I.' Though once he corrected my perhaps over-large ideas. 'Do not grant me omniscience!' said he. 'Where I focus there I am.'

This condition of ubiquity was explained as being 'the central theme of my being. I live thus,' said he. Where there were those he loved or sought to help, there was he. He spoke of 'My family. . . .' and showed that these human beings had been connected in a group by ties of love over the centuries. This was the expanded living of a man who had conquered human form.

The core of his teaching was that the Rays of God permeated all things. They were ever offered. It was for us to gain intunement with them.

'Providence is the Beam. Merit is the method of attracting it.'

He taught that meditation is the 'method of attracting it; meditation and effortful living'.

'One of the objects of my work is to show that God is to be found and gained in living rather than in segregation.'

'Life is the great educator.'

'Through experience only can we learn and enrich ourselves.'

'Responsibility for our lives and our future is ours alone.'

I knew of course that during those early years of my seeking, the impulsion which I had sensed had come from this Teacher in the planes Beyond.

My experimenting had been guided by him. He had caused my finding.

His comments were always illustrative of the working of the spiritual Powers, as for instance his crisp comment once that I seemed to him 'like a trolley bus which has its hands upon the power lines overhead'!

A favourite saying was, 'God alone *is*; we are cells in His being.'

'In meditation you are taking your pitcher to be filled at the ever-flowing Spring.'

Once he whispered, to stay my attempt to rush the Heights in meditation, 'Ascend slowly. If you seek to mount too swiftly you cannot sustain the altitude.'

One of the keynotes of his teaching was, 'Man must strive to allow God to function in him.'

Inherent in his presence and his teaching was the fact that, 'The love and mercy of God is translated into human terms through the loving service of the Guardian Spirits.'

He himself was proof of this. He said, 'You are cherished beyond your knowing.'

And so I learned the *fact* of the power and presence of the Celestial Hierarchy in the inner dimensions of Being. These, as I was fortunate to be taught by one of their number, were men and women who had made the grade, who had conquered the gravitational pull of the Earth, which is the bedrock of what men call 'evil'. They had so filled themselves with the lifting forces of holy Spirit that like balloons filled and expanded with gas they had gained their release.

'Only what is stronger than gravity frees,' said he. They had disentangled their roots from the down-drag of Earth and all it stands for, and made the Holy Heights their Eternal Home. From there they operate a celestial staff-work, a service towards humanity and in particular those they love and with whom they have been associated in times gone by. They are the conductors of the power of God. It is they who use the Divine forces of Spirit, and love and mercy and wisdom of God which is now theirs, to cherish us little things on Earth. They are 'the right hand of God' and seek to make us this too.

I saw that evil is merely the pull of a previous stage of cosmic evolution; the stage left behind, like the mud at the bottom of a river from which tadpoles have risen, when they jump as frogs out into the sunshine on the river bank.

This planet itself is of the previous stage of cosmic development. We, growing upon sunlight and the realms of Spirit are developing upwards away from Earth. Its gravitational pull holds us back; our roots are still in the soil but our heads are in the air. Our hearts and minds lift upwards. The energies of which Earth is made are the enemies of Light. They clutch us, holding us down to sloth and brutishness. The updrawing of the light of the sun and of God is our saving grace. It conquers inevitably the down-drag of Earth if we let it.

He showed in many ways how the celestial Hierarchy works for us, carrying the 'saving grace' to us. He summed up his teaching in many vigorous aphorisms.

Of self-sacrifice he said, 'He who has the Spirit within him gives up all rights in himself.'

And, 'Stand aside and let the Spirit shine.'

Of love he said, 'Loving and *being* the Light carries you through the cloud which hides the Light from your vision.'

Of the highest forms of art once he said, 'Often it happens that the poet warms himself at the Spirit's fire, thus combining himself with That which he desires.'

Often I felt frightened and overwhelmed, for how could all that he had given be shared with others?

Of the Cosmic Christ he said, 'He is the Solar Logos. He is the Light-carrier from the Most High to Earth.'

'Christ is all teachers of the Light. Only the name changes with race and language.

'Human bottles flavour the celestial wine.'

'Participation in the agony and death of Christ does not mean the death of the man on a cross, but the entering into the renunciation of Selfhood, which is the way of the Cosmic Lord in His total giving of Himself to this – and other – planets.'

'The Christ is the key to our being – the living core of our Spirit.'

'He is the reflector of the Most High to us. As the sun reflects the Creative Powers, so does He bring God to us.'

2

Dreams were given often as explicit lessons in understanding. They were used as myths were used in ancient times, not to be taken literally but to be sifted for their inner meaning.

Often I would be jerked stark awake and then would lie still, working through the experience I had just dreamed, pulling it to pieces for the truths which had carefully been inserted into the weave. If, after an hour or so of this painstaking investigation, I had not yet unravelled it aright, my Teacher would give me words or flashes of vision which further elucidated the problem which was under survey.

I remember one such elucidation which came to me in the early stages, when I was pondering on the point on which he had just spoken: 'There is a rudiment of mind in every atom.'

He was seeking to make me see with the inner knowing the truth of the Planetary Logos, the Man of Earth, the Divine Life, impregnated into all things on Earth. So he gave me a graphic dream. I saw a multitude of little men, dwarfs such as in the 'Snow White' story. Each was of a colour and a characteristic of the many rock crystals and elements which make up the earth, such as amethyst, gold, silver and ruby. They were all grouped around and clinging to an immense circular hoop over which was stretched a material like the apparatus firemen hold covered in a blanket for a trapped person to jump into. As I watched, a Godlike Being leaped from On High into this great circle and as he leaped he appeared to melt into the beings of these rocky elements of Earth. He took on their existence and vitalized them. Divinity poured Itself into Earth conditions and set it on Fire with a new state in which was life. Thus was the evolution of the planet set in motion and life appeared.

My Mentor explained that the 'collective unconscious' of the psychologists had its base in the 'angel tribe' as he called it.

As I have shown, their energy-patterns, woven in ever-increasing complexity, are the stuff of which creation is forged. They offer themselves to the worlds as building material, just as the sun sends us its light rays. Trees and flowers and all vegetation partake of these angelic forces in their lower octaves, lower because nearer to Earth. Their elevated essences offer us the stuff of soul and mind. The Spirit is of them too, brought from the highest regions, the 'Angels, Principalities and Power', Archetypes of the Creative Forces of the Almighty.

My Teacher also showed me clearly that while the 'angelic stuff of mind', the lower elementals, and what certain races call the 'lesser deities', may form the 'collective unconscious' and therefore be responsible for throwing up certain pictures in the human mind, it cannot be the foundation of much which modern psychologists ascribe to it. The strata of mental and psychic energies which permeate nature may exude essences which give rise to patterns of thought and behaviour which are the ground plan of nature, but they cannot give forth in coherent speech human language and learning. Sometimes paranormal phenomena have been ascribed to this source quite erroneously.

3

I learned to see that these subtle energies which are the stuff of thought weave themselves into a dense though invisible substance about the Earth. This is what they call in the East the 'Akashic Records'.

Thought on all levels of being weave an effluence of 'electrical and magnetic forces' which hang in the invisible ethers like curtains of dull fire.

Thought given off by men and angels, by people on Earth and in the nearer planes of Spirit, weave this mesh. The radiations of all nature, of rock, vegetation and animals as well, all give off this energy-substance. It is like the smoke from a bonfire. This smoke, this complex gauze of energies, hangs about our Earth in patterns and designs like to the thoughts and events which gave them out.

The minds of men construct the most powerful and lasting of these curtains of invisible fire. Where happenings have been surcharged with passions and violence, then the thought-effluvia hang in denser states, cohering upon the forces of emotion which sent them forth. Thus we get 'atmospheres' around certain spots on Earth where passions have been aroused. Battlefields, castles where romantic episodes have been enacted, places like Versailles and the Tower of London, reek with the effluvia of the past. Those who are sensitive sometimes feel themselves overpowered by the aroma of these places, and this sparks forth latent memories in those who may even have been involved in the scenes enacted on that spot before; or else the Akashic record is tapped so forcibly that they read again in the invisible energies the happenings which still hang imprinted in the substance of the ethers.

Many curious occurrences are explained in this way.

Apparitions which are thought to be the spirits of those who have gone on are often no more than soulless accretions of this thought-energy, held together by the magnetism of passionate action, which seem almost solid in form and recognizable.

The Akasha hangs about our Earth as an envelope of complex mental energy which can be read by masters of the art.

'To see and to read is on the Path of Development,' said the Teacher.

Chapter Eighteen

RENEWAL OR REINCARNATION

1

Soon I was to have personal experience of the results of this realm of exploration.

It was explained to me that the Akashic Records could be used as a mine of information about the past by him who knows how to investigate.

'I flick through their files like a history book,' said my Teacher. And certain of his findings were shown to me.

Thus a new phase of the teaching was brought forward, the study of the continuity of life, which he called Renewal, and more particularly the study of the past history of certain men and women. Naturally only those who had made themselves noteworthy were able to be studied, for these were recorded in biography and portraiture.

The subject was opened in a way that took me by surprise.

I was gardening one day, planting pansies, when suddenly a name was dropped into my mind like a pebble into a well.

'This was my name when last on Earth,' added the Voice.

Excited, I fled for my bicycle and soon was cruising down the long hill into the city, bound for the reference library.

There I turned up this man. He was well known in English history though I was ignorant of any details about him.

Eagerly I read, borrowed books and took them home.

'This is not a game,' said the Teacher in the Silence. 'We will study history together and I will show you the factors which lead to progress in the human soul.'

Gradually the pattern emerged.

I saw that the progressive factor upon which all evolution is based is the unbroken continuity of each life over the centuries. As the Teacher taught me:

'The Spirit, the Ego, the "I am" grows over the ages. It is this, the individual Higher Self, which draws into it energy-charges from the complex atmosphere in which it lives, and these sparks-of-fire are the angelic Ray-forces we have been talking about earlier, qualities derived from the Mind of God.

'Thus each one on earth is born and built of the Divine. The Spirit is therefore eternal and indestructible.

'It expresses itself through various sheaths or bodies, or facets of itself. These sheaths are progressively of less perfect, less subtle fires. They are the soul and mental body, and the emotional and physical bodies. While these alter and change with time, the Ego remains constant, it remains Spirit of ever-increasing power and complexity.

'The individual Spirit increases its powers and parts by entering the state of physical living many times. He visits the School of Earth for successive periods of schooling. He enjoys sessions in the Beyond between each term of schooling, for rest, refreshment and consolidation of his gains. These periods of "free-wheeling" are long or short according to the needs of the soul, though Time functions differently upon the Higher Planes.

'Because of the down-drag of Earth it is in the nature of things that Earth exerts a magnetic attraction upon like substances. Therefore our bodies, our lesser selves react to the pull of Earth. We lean towards the tug of inertia and this has to be conquered. Our Spirits, being made of light-energies, obey the attractive upward call of the Sun, and of the inner Light Divine.

'And so we here on Earth are mid-way between two poles . . . the down-drag of inertia and the call of the Spirit Above.

'In order to conquer we must fight. In order to grow upon and towards the Light we must use effort.

'Effort generates friction among our inner energies, which ignites heat and finally light. So effort used in living catches us upwards. Like attracts like, and so the Light in us calls to the Light on High . . . and so we fill ourselves with the Light Divine.

'Were all things on Earth to be easy, then life would not need to use effort to survive, to feed itself, to conquer. So that which we call "evil", the downward pull of the Earth is really a stimulus, a blessing. It is the factor which ensures that we strive and generate in ourselves the power to lift ourselves upright, to grow and expand upon and into the planes of Spirit, of Light.

'All things cannot be done at once. It takes a considerable journey through the paths of Time to create ourselves from a speck of dust and to cause our Spirits to shine richly.

'So we live in the midst of this "two-way stretch", evil and good. We have one foot in each camp as it were. This is the origin of the theological doctrine that men are "born in original sin". This is the inevitable way of nature – we could not be born in any other way. Sin is merely ignorance, an inescapable part of life and growth. The glory within us will lead us upwards. Our feet may be in the mire, but our hearts and souls are made of Light Divine, and these should be listened to and obeyed.

'Experience is the method of growth.

'When the Ego has learned the lessons which only Earth-living can present to it, when it has combined the qualities to be gained on Earth into itself, then it transcends Earth conditions. It is so light-filled that it can no longer inhabit a physical body and so it rises into the heights of Spirit, it purifies, transmutes and balances the qualities which it has taken into itself, it finally transcends its soul condition, shakes off its localized soul-form and lives as expanded Spirit.

'This may take a very long time indeed.

'Knowledge of the way accelerates the power to progress.

'When we know how to climb the glassy mountain we make greater speed upwards.'

2

'The Higher Self or Ego, the Spirit of a man, contains a record of all that he has ever been.

'We have to recognize that though the Spirit is the most perfect part of a man, being of the inner Divine Fires, it is only perfect in embryo.

'A small piece of silver is perfect silver, but it has not the perfection of a work of art. It is not a Benvenuto Cellini creation. So is the Spirit of man perfect only in essence. Time will enrich its capacity, content, form and balance.

'This is what we are all engaged in doing now.

'We must use ourselves consciously, work upon ourselves, "breathe, polish, shine and seek to mend. . . ."

'Only after long years will the perfect work of art, the goldsmith's work in silver gilt, be fit to deck the Halls of Heavenly living for ever.

'The Spirit grows eternally.

'As we live, as we fight and struggle with ourselves, so do we expand and enrich our Higher Selves upon a complexity of the Divine Powers.

'Life itself is the great educator.

'So we should live richly, even dangerously, in order to give ourselves opportunity to grow.

'The essences which are indelibly compounded in the Spirit-record, which *are* the Spirit, express themselves outwards through the soul into the personality. They show themselves in predispositions, likes and dislikes, skills and aptitudes, fears and ambitions, sensitivity to beauty, the possession of "taste", comprehension of Truth and love of the Divine. All that the Ego has ever been is balanced in the composition of his Spirit, and the consequent energy-charges given outwards show in his personality and way of living.

'Psychological defects are the result of imbalance in the inner levels. Mistakes in his past lives cause knots and tangles in the energy-changes which form his soul. These show outwardly in follies and fears, neuroses of all kinds.

'Life will cure them one by one.

'These knots and tangles, these energy-charges which display imbalance, draw to themselves events of like kind, which events impinging upon the energy-knots in the psyche, release the tension, the charge of energy, and so smooth away the seat of the trouble. Life will inevitably do this for us. It is the working of the Law of Karma, the Law of Merit and Demerit.

'Faults – or imbalances – in the electrical and spiritual make-up of a person draw to them events which smooth out the tangles. These act as a salve to the distorted part in the psyche, and thenceforward the soul marches onwards free of that burden. Henceforth that type of event will no longer touch him for he has learned that lesson.

'We might ask: "Why should we know about this fact of Renewal?" The answer is clear. It teaches us our total responsibility for ourselves and our lives. When we know the method of progress, when we understand beyond doubt that flaws in our make-up inevitably draw to us misfortunes, lessons which if not learned now, must be faced and conquered eventually, then we are given impetus to control and correct ourselves, to work upon ourselves now, and so earn our joys in the future. Who will risk the false step, the easy path, once this is understood?

'Once we establish this fact of progression, everyone of us will watch our steps as a man cautiously crosses a flood upon broken ice floes.

'In the Law of Merit these knots of unbalanced energies in the psyche are regarded as debts which must be paid. The suffering involved in the working through of the experience releases this accretion of faulty energies in the soul, and so the debt is paid. The Law of Karma is not that of punishment of a wrathful God, but the necessity of the natural releasing of accretions of energy which, knotted in the personality, will hold up progress. Therefore this is the working of justice and mercy, it is a sweet-working law of liberation of past faults due to ignorance.

'Every day and hour we come up against opportunities to discharge these debts. It is wisdom not to let these chances go by.'

3

Under the Teacher's guidance I learned to see the powers of Free Will and Predestination in their true proportion.

Since the content of the Spirit-record gives off certain energy-charges which are due to actions taken by that soul in his past lives, plainly there is an element of predestination in his life. But this element is there as result and not cause. He thinks and acts in this or that way because of what he has made of himself in the past.

This is true. But nevertheless the soul who has become perceptive and self-aware, who can use the powers of reflection and self-analysis, is able to control his reaction to the personality's promptings.

This is free will.

Free will predominates in the fully conscious and mature human being, though sometimes he is taken off his guard.

The individual Higher Self shines through the soul and personality, its outer sheathes, giving of its past. Its personality is its outward form only, the mask which is compounded of the lesser energies of physical living, influenced by heredity and environment.

The Spirit has to struggle with these disadvantages. It has been born of the parents whose overall chemical and energy-content approximate his own, or which offers him a suitable entrance into physical living. The environmental conditions will give him the opportunities he needs to conquer and to grow. Debts incurred in past lives are to be paid through working through of relationships renewed in this life. Errors in the past may be adjusted now, or we must come back to them again, in some distant future.

The purpose of this life is to clear our debts, discharge our obligations to those with whom we have been involved in the past, and so go on free of the downward pull of the faults and errors which clutter our souls and Spirits, and cause them to lose altitude like sand in a balloon. It is to enrich our Selves with an abundance of the gifts of the Spirit, to love and fill ourselves with love. This will give us wings of light which will allow us our release.

The soul filled with an abundance and a balance of the Divine qualities can no longer inhabit the 'diver's boots' of a physical body which is clamped to Earth.

The energy-charges which we generate within ourselves through our habits of thought and action are either positive and winging or negative and inert.

Contact with the Light clarifies and conquers and lifts.

This Karmic Law of Debt and Repayment operates through families and nations as well as in personal relationships.

We are born into the family and the nation whose Karmic qualities will help us to learn the lessons needed. Events drawn to that nation by their own past thoughts and actions will purge and purify, sweeten and transmute the essences of our soul, if we allow it.

For we can use happiness or suffering wisely or unwisely. We can use great suffering to set us free.

There is the functioning of the Law of Magnetic Attraction or Love which gives delight to us all.

The tie of love is never broken.

It is the working of the Law of Magentism which draws to

us 'with hoops of steel' those whom we love or have lived with in friendship.

We move onwards through the spheres both here and in the Hereafter amongst those whom we love and hold dear. We are the magnets who draw to us in unbroken hold those who react lovingly to our call.

In successive lives we meet and join with those who are dear with us. Consequently we often feel the throb of warm recognition when we meet a 'new' long-lost friend.

This is the fact behind 'love at first sight' or immediate friendship. It is really a love which is as old for us as time.

4

Now I began to discover a new ability. My eyes began to see into the inner levels. I found, just as when I had watched the changes which took place over the face of Pippa when the Teacher used her, that occasionally I could see the past selves of others, if I sat quiet and watched.

Though these two cases were not true parallels, for the Teacher while using Pippa had, by an intense act of will, formed a 'mask' as he called it, in the ether over the face of Pippa, bodying forth the image of some personage that *he* had been in times gone by. Thus I saw what he presented to me. But in the case of my own opening of the eyes, I saw the past selves of certain people (who co-operated by sitting still and quiet) as they themselves had been in past centuries.

Thus my first experience in this wise was the study of a number of the notables whom my Teacher had been in centuries past. These I studied in history and biography under his guidance, until I began to grasp some of the factors which guide and control the progress of the soul.

Then I studied the face of my husband.

As I watched, several faces that still were plainly him, portrayals of his soul, flickered before my eyes. I grew to recognize that the bone-formation of face and head remained characteristic and similar. The shape of the features changed a little from century to century, especially when there was a change in race or parentage. Yet it was notably and often strikingly similar to the cast of features now worn by the soul.

This disposed of the modern argument that we are simply a product of our parentage and environment. I was taught that they were ours because of what we had been and were up to the time of conception, and their effect upon us was slight.

It is the soul which controls all, its birth, its reaction to environment, even the burden, in normal circumstances, of its parents' physical contribution.

Watching my husband I noted the same features, time and again, encasing the same soul which looked through the eyes, but with a difference. The facial effluence altered. At first I saw a leaner, harder, more hawk-like look, with a look of fierce action bitten into the bone. This was a product of time and manners, mood, psychological circumstances and present troubles. The hair, of course, was cut and set differently, there was more or less flesh according to national eating habits. Yet, fascinatingly enough, always there was the same nuance of character, the same soul effluence – with a difference.

And the difference was a conspicuous softening and sweetening from life to life. A more gentle mien finally settled on the face, an expression more *douce* and giving.

Thus was presented before my eyes the progress of a soul.

Then I turned to myself.

Acting still on instruction of course, I would sit before the mirror.

I think things happened only when my Teacher helped me, for often I saw no change at all.

But sometimes the miracle would happen.

At first I saw my own face, indeed the whole head, begin to shimmer and move, as though made of dancing electrical particles. Then as I watched, my eyes would begin to feel thick and heavy and then the apparition before me in the mirror would fade and go quite black. If I held stillness and absolute thoughtless concentration in the midst of that blackness would appear a new face, a new person, like mine yet different. The shape of head was the same, the features sometimes smaller, the eyes set differently, the hair of another mode and colour, yet always I could see the 'I am' of me showing through. There was a recognizable similarity in spite of the slight differences of features.

'Who was she and she and she?' of course I asked.

Gradually I was told.

And so began another study, the story of my own soul.

Let no one think this is all cakes and jam. It is alarming and even horrifying to realize the things one has done, the mistakes made, the foolishnesses, the faults, the weaknesses that have gone into one's make-up in the past.

And oh, the anxiety to make amends when once one realizes the inexorable law of growth, while there is time and opportunity.

From this point the study took a broader turn. Turning from the personal studies of ourselves and those nearest and dearest to us, the Teacher showed me certain lives of a number of well-known people.

At first I wished to know how he arrived at this knowledge. For I noticed that without his instruction I could not tell who were the characters shown me over the face of my husband, or in the fluctuating appearances emerging from the blankness in my own mirror. I saw different modes but could not tell their names.

He explained carefully, as usual with presentations of flashed vision on the screen of my mind, as well as in clear conversation.

It was shown me how the Spirit of a man contains a record in energy-charges of all that he has ever been and done. I used the simile earlier of a gramophone record which registers in circles of vibrations a musical symphony. Each circle may be likened metaphorically to a life of the individual. If we wish to play a few bars of the symphony we place the needle on the groove where the music is recorded. In something the same way, if we wish to read a passage in a person's past life, a master-mind can operate the focus of his perception upon a point in the Spirit-record of the man under investigation. This throws up to the surface pictures of that part of the soul's life. He watches, reads and diagnoses.

It was also likened to a great tree cut in half, whose past life is registered in the rings of its trunk. The rings which represent each year of its life may be counted and especially verdant years noted by the swelling of the bark rings.

Thus we all carry around with us the history of our age-long past, circled around us in our Spirit-form. This can be read by an adept at this study.

'Yet it is well to remember,' interpolated the Teacher, 'that the "I am" is a vortex spiralling into Infinity. It is divine stuff, it is of God.'

Confronted with this investigation immediately one is faced with one's own inadequacy, one's own ignorance. It is essential to realize that this is the life-long study of a master-mind in the Beyond, and not to be come at by light approach or hopeful guessing. Hunches do not pay. They are always wrong, and no investigator is worthy of his salt who uses guesswork. I was forced to use the strictest discipline with myself, curb my curiosity and refuse to allow my mind to speculate or wander wonderingly over the faces of my friends. Either I would be told about them in words clear and irrefutable, or I knew nothing, and so it must rest. Guesswork is both dangerous and dishonest.

So I knew that I must play the game strictly according to the rules and await instruction, never force one's imagination or listen to vague impressions.

The method of teaching me was thus: Quite simply, I did not think or wonder about a person at all. I waited until word was spoken to me quite clearly as to who a certain person had been in a past life. If no word came, then I must not speculate. When it did come, it was spoken forcibly into my ear while I was occupied in some workaday affairs, thinking of something else. Or perhaps I was walking out with my dogs, or shopping in the city. Suddenly the words would be spoken, as on the first occasion while gardening, and a new study opened up.

'So-and-so. . . .' a man in a past century, would be named as having been one of the past lives of 'So-and-so' who lived now.

Often I had no idea as to who this historical character was, neither his date nor nationality. Not being a student of history it was necessary to seek him out. So I resorted to the reference library or second-hand book shops to find out this man's story.

As time went on I was told to make a collection of historical portraits, for in this could also be instruction.

And lo, I found that comparison between a man as he is now and as he was a century ago would reveal a close resemblance to the personality-mask which was worn over the soul on both occasions.

Why? I indented for instruction into the Within.

'Because we are the product of our custom of thought, our reaction to circumstances. We forge ourselves by our way of thinking, both conscious and subconscious, and build ourselves, our bone structure upon the Ray-energies thus drawn into us. We sculpture ourselves over the ages. Change is very gradual.'

Furthermore, I found that frequently the characteristics, predispositions, faults and tendencies of the two men under review would be similar. Because the same Spirit shone out through the personality the effect of its inner ingredients, so did these twain often react in a similar fashion to experience. Because of this factor also, they tended to draw to themselves similar occurrences.

The man with boastful pride and power-lust would lose his head time and again, until the soul had learned its lesson and pride was subdued and softened into a natural humbleness of purpose.

Thus does life teach us.

Modern psychology has removed from men and women the sense of responsibility for their character and actions. We are told that our waywardness is the fault of heredity and environment. But in this new science I learned that the reverse was the case. We are entirely responsible, not only for our personality and characteristics but for much of what comes to us in the path of life. There is justice and loving wisdom in all that happens, for life proceeds in stately majesty according to the Laws of Cause and Effect, and is not capricious and buffeted by chance.

As I studied the growing collection of personalities who lived both now and aforetime certain laws and human patterns of behaviour came to light.

Chapter Nineteen

THE PATH OF A SOUL

As time went on I was given the opportunity to study the path of a single soul in certain of its aspects . . . that of my celestial Teacher. Thus I could observe the way things tended to happen. Discretion forbids the giving of his actual names in each life, but one can discern the general trend which is typical of the development in certain types.

Firstly it is noticeable that some souls, from the commencement of their journey in human form – and before – have a way of drawing more greedily upon the Powers Divine than most. Like the man who, because he has formed the habit of deep breathing, has developed a powerful frame, a deep chest and massive lungs and heart cage . . . so does the man who draws deeply upon the Powers of the Spirit create within himself a powerful soul. This practice may be conscious or unconscious. Indeed, I have known it in some animals, who because of this grow too big for their breed and are radiant in character and giving.

We may start our observations at a time not too far distant, say some 2,500 years ago when historical records are available to pick up this soul's activities. We could probe further back, into biblical times and the period of the Pharaohs, but this tends to smack of fantasy so I will resist the temptation.

He first erupts onto the stage of European history as a Greek. He was a warrior chieftain of brilliant abilities but somewhat uncertain character. Of abounding vitality and optimism, capricious, splendid in appearance, brave as a lion, for ever getting himself into scrapes but always extricating himself with seemingly incredible luck, popular, adored by his associates, hated by those who found his ebullience troublesome; always sun-filled like Apollo and laughing at fate and fortune. A turn for philosophy and the search for truth was always with him. He felt the inner Fire which called him. After what seemed to be a charmed and

THE PATH OF A SOUL

successful life he met a violent end at the hands of his enemies. His folly eventually punctured his splendid radiation which was his protection through many dangers and difficulties.

For several lives this pattern was repeated. Always the warrior, always the leader, often the chieftain or king, always the conqueror in many campaigns and loved by his followers, yet the chink in his armour of radiant protection was ever there. The adversary caught him in the end through insurrection, by some ruse wasteful of life, or seeming accident. Always he outreached himself, his vision being stronger than his power of personal protection, while his weakness with the opposite sex built up Karmic debts against him. These penetrated his spiritual armour and he fell.

As time went on the character changed. The lessons of living, hard and terrible, gradually were learned. He developed a predisposition towards order and reform. No one knew better than he the heavy cost of rebellion against established order. These lessons were dyed in the wool, as it were. He had learned them through suffering and loss in the past. Henceforth he was a protagonist and passionate defender as well as instigator of order and justice, of fair play for all men, high or low, of the civilized life, of education and culture in all its forms.

His sense of the inner Fire called him inwards, the truth of his intuition teaching him. He became the philosopher monarch. Gentler, more introspective, but always the powerful rod for the vandal, always defender of the City of God, the centre of civilized order among men.

His passion for rule and reform, his majesty of purpose, led him to be born frequently to the royal purple. His sense of justice made him the good king. His centuries of experience as a warrior made him the victorious planner of campaigns and leader of Christendom against attack. Plainly he was often called into service by the Powers Above, to be a Guardian of mankind, to help to spread progress and a civilized way of life. He lived in Rome, in Gaul, in England.

Always his radiance of the inner Fire called forth envy and hatred from those who preferred disorder and darkness, always the negative powers were ranged against him. But his visions and his plans conquered and helped to carry the torch of civilization forward over the known world.

Wide experience imprinted deep in the soul and Spirit gave him the inner knowing, though many mistakes were inevitably made, and gradually the cut and thrust of the warrior's life became more gentle. He turned to the life of the Spirit. He became poet and singer of truth and marvellous with his pen in expressing the truths of God. The quiet life became his love.

The Church put a hand upon him and called him to her service – as he had often defended her in the past.

This time the greatest sacrifice was demanded of him. Rather than forswear his own deep beliefs and all he stood for in religious faith, he died at the stake.

This terrible experience purified the soul. But it was not his last appearance on Earth. One more life was allowed him . . . a life of happiness and fulfilment. He became a poet of subtlest turns of thought, delighting when young in prankish adventure. He loved and married. He became an honoured dignitary of the Church, he became a philosopher of unusual intellectual powers, straining at the knot of truth. He became a leader of man's thought – and still is.

From that point he gained his liberty in the Realms Above – thinker into the New Age.

Chapter Twenty

FLASHBACKS

'Flashbacks' came to me from time to time, and still do. Were these sorts of experiences to be understood and legitimatized, it might be that many others would come forward with like experiences to relate.

They are a sudden reappearance before the screen of the mind's eye, of a scene in one's past history.

It is logical that this should happen, since it is the way of ordinary memory, through the association of ideas, to throw up pictures of scenes in which we have been involved in this life.

But flashbacks, as they might be called, have a quality of reality which is not present in the ordinary memory pictures which normally appear in the mind. They are more vivid, they have the appearance of *present* reality, and they are always in colour. In fact, it seems as though one were really *there*, and not merely remembering or observing the scene from a distance.

Many of us experience these almost without remark. It is, dare I say it, a not unusual phenomenon of childhood. Children are so much nearer to the inner levels. Much of their play takes place in contact with the inner dimensions. Solitude increases this ability to withdraw into inner levels of being, and the lonely child in imagination frequently turns back into these curtains of time for interest and solace. In the East it is not considered to be fantasy or madness to give forth memories of a past life, and indeed it is in some countries of the East – as for instance in Tibet – the normal thing. Gradually, as the child grows up and accustoms itself to its new surroundings and life-condition, its interest is gripped, the soul leans forward, as it were, into its present surroundings so that memories of its past life fade.

But in many of us, unremarked, an association of ideas can operate the link-up, the recall of earlier selves that we have been, earlier episodes in our unbroken life-history. In these cases, usually the atmosphere of the half-remembered events hangs round us, but names and places are not forthcoming. To find out these we need the help of a Teacher.

I remember one such which took me when I was about six years old, which will serve as example.

At the time I could not explain it to myself at all.

I was to have two teeth out which threatened to crowd the mouth as I grew. I went with my mother to the dentist knowing that I was to have gas. I was filled with a dreadful sense of horror and foreboding. The dentist's waiting room was on the first floor and while my mother sat idly turning over the pages of a magazine little knowing my fear, I took to pacing up and down the room. I thought at the time, with the 'observer-me', that this was a very 'un-little-girl-like' way to behave. One did not make such a fuss about having out a couple of teeth, but somehow this was different. I knew I could not submit myself to the power of a man leaning over me. If I did I was lost.

Keeping my thoughts to myself I stormed up and down in a state of ominous terror, and then stopped to look out of the window. It was a grey, icy day, early in the year, and a dull gloom hung over everything and a curious dark stillness pervaded the room. I looked down on the heads of the passers by and then fear took me. I knew that my life was at stake.

The door opened and, followed by my mother, I was ushered into the surgery. It was as I feared . . . there were two men there, not one (for a doctor was in attendance), and certain that they meant my death I screamed.

My mother's quelling look sobered me and I sank into the chair and in a moment lost consciousness.

The sequel to this happened only two or three years ago.

I had been staying in Essex and arrived in London at Fenchurch Street Station on my way to a Refugee Committee Meeting.

I had an hour or so to wait, so I decided to wander through the Tower of London, a place I had not visited for very many years.

I joined a group of sight-seers who were following a Warder clad in his Tudor costume up to Tower Green. We all stood around the place where the block had stood while he expatiated. It was a cold grey, shivery sort of day. I felt uneasy and glanced away to my left where there was a row of small houses within the precincts, where, said the Warder, certain prisoners had awaited execution. Suddenly the terror was over me again, and there was an appalling stench as of an abattoir in my nostrils. That long-forgotten incident at the dentist's merged with a deeper memory. I was again looking down from an upstairs room — awaiting my own execution. Panic mounted and I felt the horror of men standing over me and I knew that they were there to do me to death.

It was all day before that sense of doom and the horrible stench faded from the forefront of my mind and I was fully back in this century.

In this way are many of childhood's terrors explained.

Such experiences in our past lives make so deep an imprint upon the deep subconscious that they tend to throw up shadows from time to time. Sometimes the whole incident comes forward, with oneself as principal actor, and either a mild form of *déja-vu* is experienced, or else one is plunged into a re-enactment of a past reality.

Now having disgorged, as it were, this subconscious dread of being in another's power, that episode, but a few minutes in a life of many centuries, will no longer trouble me.

I recount this as it may help others to understand their own secret fears.

Chapter Twenty-one

OPPORTUNITY AND PLANS

1

The Teacher had made it clear from the beginning that what I was being given was not for me alone, that I must find means of giving it out again. Into the silence of my mind he had said, 'Religion is the science of ballistics. A religious understanding helps people to "take off".'

It was plain that lack of a true understanding and a consequent bleak scepticism and loss of way is bedevilling our age, and puncturing the sense of purpose which should carry the race forward and help it to be 'airborne'.

But how could I give out what I had been given? I lived amongst those of traditional and orthodox background and they would certainly think me not only presumptuous in the highest degree but mad. So the problem ate into me for years and I felt suffocated with the longing and urge to share with others what I had learned and how it had come to me, for surely in this there was such rich promise for all people. But still I said nothing to any but a handful of intimate friends, not knowing where to start nor how to begin.

It took a very long while to find a channel for offering something of what I had gleaned in the inner school of teaching. However, meanwhile this gave me time to continue to learn and to digest this philosophy.

There was so much to be learned, and the 'encyclopaedia of the Spirit' opened its pages to me only in accordance with my ability to probe and to question.

Eventually, in a way which I had long learned to regard as 'celestial staff-work', a windfall brought me a sum of money as an unexpected gift, and with this, in 1953, I started a small spiritual journal. I called it *Wisdom*, using the same *nom-de-plume*, 'Armido'. I wrote and edited it myself, given confidence

OPPORTUNITY AND PLANS

by the knowledge that the Teacher was with me, helping day by day. So I found a certain liberation in this work, together with much interest in the correspondence it brought me. Another magazine gave me a friendly write-up, and so I prospered for some time. However, printing costs rose, and so after two or three years my capital was at an end and I withdrew from publication. But this effort had taught me one thing, the deep thirst that was felt by very many for spiritual understanding beyond what was offered by the Churches.

Then one day, in the summer of 1956, thirteen years after the Teacher had last used the physical instrument of Pippa to speak to me, suddenly he came again.

Pippa was staying with us again, and she and I were doing the flowers in the drawing room one sunny day, when suddenly he was there. Pippa was propelled to a chair and with the usual sign he spoke.

In plain words which reverberated through the room I was told it was high time I spoke out, time I ceased using the camouflage of a *nom-de-plume*, time I told the story plainly, which had not been brought for me alone.

Abashed I murmured that I did not feel equal to speaking out, nor knew how or to whom.

'Quench this crippling modesty,' he said firmly. 'You must cease to conceal the light under the bushel of your diffidence. It is not for you to assess suitability. Forget the self. Let the teaching speak. Stand aside and let the light shine.'

And oh, the stimulus and courage given by those words spoken so forcibly and with so much authority.

Shortly after this at last a suitable occasion offered.

I became acquainted with members of a society lately formed for the Study of ESP and psychics. It was called then the Churches Fellowship for Psychical Study, but they later added to this title the words 'for Spiritual Studies'. Here I found intelligent people, religious, and of a seeking mind, and I was invited to speak to them. At last I told the story of the celestial Visitor, and something of what I had learned in this way.

I realized then why the Teacher had again used the physical instrument of Pippa in order to make clear to me in words which hit upon the outer ear the need to speak out fearlessly. Plainly he knew of the sympathetic audience which was coming into view, and he wished to help me to achieve confidence, and to make sure that I would not, cowardly, miss the outlet engineered for me.

2

It occurs to me that in this chronicle of my spiritual adventuring I have said little about my reaction at that time to the Church itself. While this is chiefly because I have written at length on the subject in my last book, *The Fire of Knowing*,[1] it may be of interest in this connection to report an event which took place about this time.

While I have always felt a pull of tenderness towards the Church, yet usually, when I attended a service, I found myself deeply distressed by some facets of what took place there. So often it seemed as though clergy and congregation were quite unnoticing of the words they repeated, and the meaning of the hymns and psalms they chanted. How came they to believe that these primitive and fierce sentiments were expressions of the Will and Mind of God? Presumably long custom had dulled their sense of meaning.

Of late years many frank commentaries have appeared, showing the public concern at certain of the sentiments contained in the psalms and readings, but in those days I had not heard a word of indignation. How one longed that the lovely cathedrals and village churches, whose architecture at least appealed as expressions of the Divine, once more should be centres for the distillation of the riches of spiritual wisdom. Yet inevitably each service that I attended sent me away distressed at the emptiness of much that was offered and at the wasted opportunity. So I had for some years visited the beautiful churches only when they were empty, and it was possible to sit and absorb the atmosphere undisturbed.

One day I was in London, where, as Area Representative for the Save the Children Fund – for Refugees – I had attended a Conference at Church House, Westminster. After the meeting was over I wandered into Westminster Abbey. Evensong was in progress. Half a dozen or so people sat in the main body of the church and I took a seat behind a young couple, interested to

[1] Vol. III of the Trilogy, *The Science of Wisdom*.

OPPORTUNITY AND PLANS

find them there. The singing finished, invisible and almost inaudible behind the great screen, and with a grating sound the loudspeaker was switched on for the reading of the lesson.

We heard the story of Esther. We learned how King Ahasuerus, irritated because his wife Vashti had refused to come to Court at his bidding, sent his men out to the villages round about to search for beautiful maidens. When found, a great number of these young girls were brought to the palace for the King's pleasure. We heard how the Court officials kept the girls for a year, cleansed and perfumed them and sent them each evening one by one into the King's chamber. If the King delighted in her the girl was called by name and retained in the palace. If not, she was sent home. Esther was one of these girls. Being obedient to her guardian she took her turn. The King found pleasure in Esther and kept her by him, and set her on the throne in place of Vashti, his wife. Finally we heard how Esther procured the hanging of the King's minister and his ten sons, with the consequent safety of her own people. 'Here endeth the first Lesson,' boomed the loudspeaker.

The young couple in the pew in front of me looked at one another with raised eyebrows. Is this the Church's precedent for divorce? they seemed to be thinking.

I felt a sort of electrification like a lightning thrust within me. Rage boiled up . . . oh, the wasted opportunity and the disgrace of what was offered. I felt that my rage must boil over.

I waited until the procession of choir and clergy came later down the aisle and then I rose and went to the door of the vestry. I begged the verger to ask the Dean, whom I recognized, to come and speak with me.

The Dean came, a query on his face.

'Will you be so good as to tell me,' I asked with mounting passion, '*what* was the spiritual lesson in your reading this evening?'

The Dean looked startled.

'Oh yes, I see what you mean,' he answered. 'I know, it is a new translation we are trying out. And anyway, you know, oriental potentates did behave like that.'

'Surely,' I cried, 'the fact that oriental potentates behaved like that is beside the point. Tell me what was the spiritual message in the lesson!'

The Dean gave in.

'Well, what can I do,' he said apologetically. 'I have to read it, it is in the Calendar.'

'No wonder,' said I, 'that this lovely Abbey is nearly empty, when all that was offered was such stuff.' I told him of the young couple, so modestly come in for food of the Spirit to this mighty hub of a Christian country, and what was offered them was a dish of pornography.

Behind my rage I was sorry for the Dean. It was not his fault. The fault lay at all our doors that this should be permitted the length and breadth of the country. The fact that we had outgrown this primitive approach to religious thought had not yet found acceptance, and what our fathers had sanctioned was still right for most of us. Finally I left the poor man, hoping I had not hurt him too much.

3

Since the first coming of the Teacher from the Beyond there had been growing in my mind, at his instigation, the idea of the need to form a Centre for spiritual teaching. It would be a sort of 'University of the Spirit', to counteract the logical positive and materialistic teachings with which our academic universities abound, where the young are often indoctrinated with the inflexible scepticism of their tutors. Their fresh young openness to learn and their innate sense of the magic behind all things becomes blunted by contact with the thought of those who are filled with book-learning, but with no conviction of the heart.

The world is in a sorry state in this transition period. Mass desertion from the churches, the mental hospitals overflowing, crime spreading and the young, some of them, seeming to have completely lost touch with the spirit, the purpose, the goal of living, and the way of achievement.

What could be offered to bridge the gap between the world of matter, of material values, and the world of Spirit? The old language of conventional religion no longer speaks to our people. The young turn away perplexed.

It seems that the only salve lies within ourselves.

Only through our own experiences can we come to an inner certainty of the Divine Fire. In past centuries we have – most of us – relied upon the authority of the Church, its scriptures, its teachings, to enrich our solitary hours, to keep us in touch with the essence of life.

Now we have lost touch and people have lost the way inwards.

Without this contact, this breathing of the inner perfume of Spirit, men lose hope, grow faint-hearted and go under to the strain of living. Their nerves give way. They are like a dog without a master and the knowledge of home, food and warm fire behind them; they become, in the secret recesses of their minds, waifs in eternity.

I visualized a kind of Lay Monastery; indeed, there need to be many up and down the land, to which people can go to find the inner Self and a sense of closeness to the spirit of things. To be rejoined, connected up with the Heart of the Universe, through the practice of meditation and a new understanding.

It is now as though the vine has lost touch with the branches, the blossoms are falling off for lack of the distillations of the Spirit. They need to find the way back, young and old alike.

I saw our University of the Spirit, our Lay-Monastery, as a place of beauty, in natural surroundings of peace and verdant green, apart from the world; away from airways, the noises of the high roads and the racket of commerce.

Here would be quiet. Here would be all the riches of the Spirit. Here would be silence.

We would give teaching in the Laws of the Spirit, we would help towards a fresh outlook, a sense of the oneness, the interdependence of all life. I remembered the Teacher's words in the Silence: 'Every cubic centimetre is shot through with all that is.' This we would teach, that contact could only be gained through the Within.

All the fear, all the noise, all the nervous tensions of the world are reacting round and around, and the sense of loss, of spiritual dislocation undermines the people's normal potency.

Here would be the practice of meditation, carefully taught. Men and women need to find their own stairway to the inner Divine. No one can accept it at second hand any longer. Each must find his own experience of God. Once found, he has achieved an inner knowing of the sustaining power, the light, the joy of the Spirit. The age of faith alone is over. We need a knowing.

We would offer a relaxation in woods and fields, with time for silence. We would offer music and the glory of art, pictures of the first order, drama that was of spiritual interest, poetry that resonated with the wealth that lies at the heart of things.

A period spent in this place would renew the soul and send it forth strengthened.

And so I set about planning.

In order to plan one must visualize. So using this picturing of our need, a beginning was made.

Roselaleham was found overnight. It was perfect for our purpose, more spacious than our last home, standing in some acres of garden and woodland. It was in exactly the circumstances of peace and beauty envisaged. It became our new home high in unspoilt loveliness upon the Devon hills.

And thus our work started.

Chapter Twenty-two

FULFILMENT

1

By this time I had written a Trilogy called *The Science of Wisdom*, published under my own name by Sidgwick and Jackson. I felt at last that something was getting done.

But then I had a setback. It was a hitch in my own confidence. I happened to pick up Volume II of my Trilogy and I was instantly struck with its inadequacy. I suddenly realized anew how totally insufficient I was for this task. Whereas I had thought earlier that I should be inspired to give the vision as it had been given to me, I could see now the depth of my failure. I realized that my intellect, my education, my command of words and pen were too inadequate to dare to try to use in order to lay the vision before the public. I railed at my intellectual inability. I was bitterly sorry that the Teacher had backed a loser. And yet, when one faces the truth, the truth of one's own insufficiency, in a sense one dies. In a strange way one dies and is set free. One loses hold even of the eager ambition to serve.

Then came a letter from the Bishop of Exeter. Scenting heresy in my book, he said that he had sent the book to Dr Mascal, who had the Chair of Moral Philosophy at Christ Church, Oxford. The Bishop wrote that he noticed 'what seem to be on first reading a number of verbal heresies . . . I am not convinced, however, that these are essential to the argument', he therefore was going to consult the learned Doctor at Oxford for his opinion.

In time back came a letter from Dr Mascal. He said that he considered the book 'a brilliant twentieth-century rendering of the Gnostic theory of the aeons. In fact reading it I understood for the first time what the Gnostics were getting at!'

This cheered me – as I had not read the Gnostics! And as it happened soon afterwards I was talking about my problems to a man who was a brilliant scholar, who immediately went to his shelves and took down a copy of Dante's Paradiso, and translating it from the Italian he read me the passage: 'Give the whole vision.' And he repeated: 'You must give your whole vision as an autobiography – and write it in detail forcibly. That's the way to give your philosophy.'

The words rang in my mind.

'Give the whole vision.' Perhaps one day I would do so.

But just now there was other work on hand.

My books, and the magazine which I had earlier sent out, followed by talks which I had been giving at Roselaleham and to various other societies, had drawn around us a number of like seeking minds. So the time was plainly come to launch out. With a handful of kindred spirits of similar enthusiasm we formed a Trust and announced our first Summer Conference. We would not wait for capital and staff and a mansion large enough to accommodate those who may wish to attend. We would start in our own home with what we had.

The venture succeeded beyond my wildest dreams.

Lacking a hall large enough to accommodate those who applied, we hired a great marquee with a stage, flower-decked, while caterers served refreshments. Our garden was 800 feet above the level of the lovely Exe Valley, and the rich countryside with its splendid views across to Dartmoor added a luxury of unspoilt nature to the food of the Spirit.

Dr Westall, Bishop of Crediton, with whom I had worked on Refugee Committees and who had always shown interest and sympathy in our plans, presided over and spoke at our opening session. We had invited some speakers from London whom I had recently met, who were exponents of varying aspects of what might be called 'new age thought', and I spoke as well. We started each day with instruction in simple meditation and a short practise of the silence. We had music and drama and poetry as I had long ago planned.

The week was a resounding success and many people joined the Roselaleham Trust.

During our second Summer Festival a gale sprang up in the Channel and we heard over the wireless of many marquees at church fêtes being swept away. As we listened to the high wind and rain and heard the canvas billowing, the guy ropes slapping,

I felt that we were on one of St Paul's missionary journeys, riding out the violent storm.

The structure held, but it had become apparent that a turning point had been reached. We must have a permanent conference hall for our growing number of members.

A fund was opened.

But on the last night of that Festival week, being weary, I went early to bed, anxious for the future of our work. English weather could not always be expected to co-operate with our timetable. People had been as generous as possible, but it had been my experience that those who were especially interested in the spiritual aspects of living were rarely people of substance. It was impossible to envisage the large sum needed for the building of the Hall as coming very swiftly.

But I was leaving out of account the Powers of the Spirit.

One of the rare physical phenomena was shown us.

I was lying in broad daylight looking out of my window across the splendid vista of woods and fields that sloped away from the house and out to the hills of Dartmoor, tinged with the setting sun.

On the window ledge opposite me, some fifteen feet away, were three old Worcester dessert dishes. They were part of a service which I loved for its apple green and gold design.

Then I heard words from the familiar Voice in the Silence.

'Valuable service shall soon bear fruit.' This was followed by the words: 'My power *is* here!' spoken with colossal emphasis.

Then there was a crack like a pistol shot . . . and one of the Worcester dishes leapt up a few inches into the air and landed down again in its place, split clean in half.

My husband heard the noise and came running upstairs.

We looked at each other in amazement. Then I told him the words I had heard. I was ashamed of my earlier doubts.

The *double entendre* struck us both, but we were not prepared for the swiftness of the aftermath.

The 'celestial staff-work' was as immaculate as ever.

Within a few weeks I met for the first time a man who became interested in the work of the Trust. He came to some of the meetings. Hearing of our need for a conference hall he took out his cheque book and wrote us the sum needed to pay for the hall outright.

By the following Spring our hall was in being, and at the next summer Festival our Bishop-patron dedicated it with due ceremony.

From that time onwards the Roselaleham Trust, ship of the new venture, was in constant use, with all its sails set, and the work for understanding and unity continued to spread. By the hundreds who came to the Conferences it was plain that we had struck the note for which many were eager. People were athirst for an oasis in the parched desert of materialism that was the world outside. And a note of joyous comradeship was struck amongst those who came again and again to contribute to the feast of spiritual welfare that permeated those gatherings.

For me this was fulfilment indeed.

Chapter Twenty-three
THE OPEN CHURCH

Our venture prospered, and year after year the numbers increased. Our hall was packed with over two hundred people.

It had always been my hope that the Churches would adopt the practice, this 'new look'. As I see it, the inner Truth of Christianity has become fossilized in the stony covering of ancient custom. The archaic approach is no longer suitable for the people of today.

In ancient times the attitude was different. The bulk of the 'hungry sheep' of those days used the emotional levels of the human soul, and their hearts welcomed the sweet stories and knew them to embody Truth. Nowadays, more often than not, the heart is left out of account, it is suspect as an organ for the appreciation of truth. With the advance of the race, and increased facilities for education, men and women use the mental approach. The scientific attitude has dried and intellectualized most of us. Much that is of the universal essence of Reality is regarded as superstition. Scepticism, agnosticism, even atheism reigns as never before. The old language of religion is no longer acceptable.

Psychology has taught us, erroneously, that it is 'too good to be true'. Faith has gone, and with it the old stabilizing moral values.

Laboriously, and with years of patient experiment and analysis, science is beginning to prove what to the readers of the Bible long ago would consider truisms; ESP, telepathy, 'the Voice of God'. In time it seems that scientists will be called in to prove the dimensions beyond the physical. They are verging on it now. Their probes are discovering levels of energy which can scarcely be called physical. It has been already declared by certain of the greatest scientific thinkers that the refinements of energy in the infinite atom can only be explained on the basis of *Mind*. But this will take a long while, and in the meantime the people starve and thirst and fall away from the path of development. Only contact with the Fire of the Spirit will teach them the laws of living.

The heart and soul knows its own deeps, but the intellect of the present day dare not accept the inner Truth. We have been taught to doubt, to scoff at the 'heart which has her reasons which reason herself knows not of'.

In vain do we gather before the general public on television and radio, and seek to dig into the thoughts and convictions of one another.

'What do you think?'

'What dare I believe?'

No man was ever convinced by argument. The multitude of human opinions iron one another out, and the hungry sheep are still unfed.

There is only one way to satisfy this inner craving, a craving so compulsive that the young, the foolish, seek to slake it with the artificial and lowering stimulus of drugs.

The way is through Meditation, for thus we find our own experience of the inner Divine.

In vain do we listen to the description of others. It may impress but it does not convince. The only convictions come *through our own personal experience*.

As I found for myself, the practice of meditation, the practice of the Stillness, actually leads one to the powers of the Spirit. Only thus does the soul feel fed and satisfied.

It is as exciting a search as any moon-probe, and far more so because it is limitless. It is no less than a probe into the 'fourth and fifth dimensions' of being, whither no instrument or vehicle can take you. Only the mind of man can perform this feat, within its own self-woven vehicle, for the essence of mind *is* the essence of the Divine. All things have at their heart's core the essence of mind and spirit, and only the usage of the mind and spirit in the right way can get us there. It is a miracle only in appearance. The nature of the experiment is simply the manipulating of the laws which govern life, with skill, with knowledge. And these can only be gained through patient experiment.

One must forge one's own technique. Each mind is different.

Each has a different age-long history, therefore the energies which forge each soul vary as widely as the sweet pea from the rose.

It seems that Meditation is the way towards the next step in evolution.

Our bodies are more or less perfected. Our brains, our intellects are 'express and admirable'. But we are earthbound until we forge for ourselves new instruments of knowing. Meditation sends out antennae into the next planes of being. Just as the mind and the needs of the body have created us as we are now, have created horns upon the heads of animals for protection, teeth for eating, hands for manipulation, eyes for seeing, ears for hearing, so can a new usage of the inner levels of the mind throw out lines-of-force from the head (in the invisible) which in time forge instruments of intunement with the next planes of being. With ardent practice not only do the senses of eyes and ears develop subtler levels of perception, but the mind itself penetrates into dimensions of awareness which far outstrip anything that physical science with its wonders of wireless can achieve.

It is as though hitherto we have been cool water confined to a kettle and now our spirits are on the boil, and able to escape like steam into the area around us. Our mind is in every globule of steam. This is a realm of adventure into new dimensions of being.

The artists of old, the architects, the musicians, were men of faith. With prayer and meditation Fra Angelico prepared himself to paint his murals. Contact with the Divine energies, thus induced, provided a heavenly art, a heavenly message to man, beauty caught from the planes above. This is true inspiration. Reformers, innovators of all things good, capture their ideas from the Higher Realms of thought. Those who create art simply by delving into the morass of their own subconscious tune in with and give off 'fumes of the underworld', and disharmony and ugliness results. This is what our world suffers from today.

Mind is a ubiquitous energy. It is the stuff of which all the Universe is made, on all its infinite levels of being. Cultivation of the finer levels of the mind – in each one of us – can and does link us with the Divine.

That which men – childlike still – have called 'God' down the ages, is an Ocean of Mind. Heart, soul, spirit, life, intelligence, love, light, all these are our pathetic attempts to describe the attributes of the One Supreme. Because we have in some degree these attributes ourselves, an inner knowing tells us that these are derived from the Creative Source, we are aware that the 'Bedrock of our Being' is this and infinitely more besides.

In meditation we try to still the busy material side of our natures, and seek contact with the magnificence within. We feel that there is Home, there is rest and refreshment, there is sustenance of the Spirit. And practice proves to us that it really is so. Nothing else will prove it but our own experience. Conviction only comes through personal adventuring. Only when a blind man recovers his sight and sees the light does he know what light is.

Practice makes the grade. Patience is needed, and determination such as an explorer has, a mountaineer who at last gains the heights.

The purpose of writing this book has been to try to show, as honestly as possible, that this practice does work. That it need not be attempted from the standpoint of any one religion or another. Mind is everywhere. He or That which we name 'God' is everywhere, is all and everything.

The practice of meditation is the using of the escape hatch of the water-logged submarine of ourselves, to force our exit into the sunshine above. Each in our own degree, and according to our subtle usage of the inner powers, can and will succeed. He who experiences *knows*, and is refreshed, cleansed and renewed – and filled with a splendid joy.

The proof of the champagne is the testing of it.

In our congresses at Roselaleham and amongst the many conferences and groups that are springing up all over this country, one has only to watch the faces of those who come. Tense and anxious faces turn to countenances that shine. In a few hours – or days – a wonderful difference spreads over the faces of the people, and this is expression of the gold they have found in the Silence.

Some say that they 'can't meditate'. Some take to it as easily as a bird flies. Yet all are wonderfully benefited, for there spreads through the gathering an atmosphere of peace that welcomes the light. Just as the iridescent colours of oil unite when spread upon calm water, so do the auras of the people absorb and glow with a new light, drawn from the inner levels of the Divine Beams which spread and unite one with another into a lake of spiritual Fire. Sympathy and love suffuses the whole company of kindred spirits.

This is the true basis for unity in the world.

Unity will never come from an ironing out of differences in tenets of belief and outer observance, it comes through the reaching out of the souls to the Sunlight within, and spreading it through every concourse of people. From this Light there is love, tolerance, sympathy, understanding, all those qualities of the Divine which we so sadly lack, which we need to increase in ourselves through the various techniques of creative thought and Meditation.

'As a man thinketh in his heart so he *becomes*.'

In other words, as we think, so do we send out a tuning note which links us with the beams sent out from On High. So do we fill ourselves with the spiritual Fire. For did not the same 'God', the One Supreme, the Most High, teach all the peoples of the Earth, at different times, in a manner suited to their race and development? But 'Human bottles flavour the celestial wine', so have the varying characteristics in men and races tainted the original Divine inflow of teachings.

We need to understand this and come back to a sense of the one-ness of life, for all are expressions of the Divine, at varying stages of evolution. Only thus can peace and unity come to the world.

Men need to take a step up on the path of evolution. This can only be done through the development of the mind and spirit. Through the filling of the soul with the Powers Divine, so that we shine like suns and radiate to one another a blessing with our presence.

It seems to me that the Church of the future lies in these groups, congresses and gatherings of people, be they large or small, in a lovely church or in someone's private sitting room, where it is recognized that God the One Supreme is the Giver of all religions, be it East or West. Man it is who filters the truth through his own most fallible mind. Barriers and separations between creed and creed are made by men and not by the Giver of Enlightenment.

At Roselaleham we invited those of all creeds. We had Buddhist, Sufi, Jew, Roman Catholic, Quaker, Anglican and other sects of the Christian Church, and all met upon the Divine Ground of Truth. The Open Church of the future should be thus, welcoming all as sons of the Most High.

Epilogue

Since the writing of this book my husband has suddenly gone on – with coronary thrombosis.

Because the breadwinner, the supporter of the bricks and mortar of Roselaleham has left us, sadly and with reluctance we have had to close down the Trust.

At first I was aghast, seeing our work as coming to a close. But it is a true saying that when one door closes another opens – and indeed it has proved to be the case. During the last decades many enlightened groups of people have come together to form societies and associations, adult colleges and retreat houses, where the 'New Understanding' (as it might be called) flourishes. And it has been my privilege to speak at many such Centres, both at home and abroad.

At one such College, where recently I gave a series of talks, an American visitor delivered herself thus. She said something like this:

'I do hope you English people realize that you are the leaders of the spiritual world. I have travelled a great deal and nowhere have I met anything like this in other parts of the world. You over here have the knowledge, the experience and the spiritual calibre to lead the world. Forget all this talk of second-rate nation and collapse of power. Your power is in the Spirit, in your way of life, in your tolerance, and your advanced spiritual outlook. We in my country look to you to lead us . . . and God knows the world needs spiritual leadership now as never before. God bless you all.'

GEORGE ALLEN & UNWIN LTD

Head office:
40 Museum Street, London, W.C.1
Telephone: 01-405 8577

Sales, Distribution and Accounts Departments
Park Lane, Hemel Hempstead, Herts.
Telephone: 0442 2344

Athens: 7 Stadiou Street, Athens 125
Auckland: P.O. Box 36013, Northcote Auckland 9
Barbados: P.O. Box 222, Bridgetown
Beirut: Deeb Building, Jeanne d'Arc Street
Bombay: 103/5 Fort Street, Bombay 1
Calcutta: 285J Bepin Behari Ganguli Street, Calcutta 12
P.O. Box 23134, Joubert Park, Johannesburg, South Africa
Dacca: Alico Building, 18 Montijheel, Dacca 2
Dehli: 1/18 B Asaf Ali Road, New Delhi 1
Hong Kong: 105 Wing on Mansion, 26 Hankow Road, Kowloon
Ibadan: P.O. Box 62
Karachi: Karachi Chambers, McLeod Road
Lahore: 22 Falettis' Hotel, Egerton Road
Madras: 2/18 Mount Road, Madras 2
Manila: P.O. Box 157, Quezon City D-502
Mexico: Libreria Britanica, S.A., Separio Rendon 125, Mexico 4, D.F.
Nairobi: P.O. Box 30583
Ontario: 2330 Midland Avenue, Agincourt
Rio de Janeiro: Caixa Postal 2537-Zc-00
Singapore: 36c Prinsep Street, Singapore 7
Sydney, N.S.W.: Bradbury House, 55 York Street
Tokyo: C.P.O. Box 1728, Tokyo 100-91

HARA: THE VITAL CENTRE OF MAN
KARLFRIED GRAF VON DURCKHEIM

Durckheim, the well-known philosopher and psycho-therapist, abandons the old dualistic thinking about man in terms of body and soul, which is the hallmark of Western thought. He shows how man must always be taken as one whole, the person. Realisation of the Self can never be a spiritual development alone but must include the body. It can be achieved only by 'practise' of the soul-body unity. Such practise must be based on the knowledge of the vital centre wherein division is non-existent. It was in Japan where Durckheim discovered the teaching and the tradition of Hara—Japanese for the vital centre. Through some experience of it Western man also could be freed from his persistent conceptual thinking —which inevitably blocks his access to Being—and could be put in contact with the Greater Life and so achieve that state of mind which is the pre-requisite of Self-realisation. The book, often in accord with the most recent trends in religion, philosophy and psycho-therapy, contains several illustrations and three outstanding texts by Japanese masters on Hara.

THE INWARD ODYSSEY
EDITH B. SCHNAPPER

In the sacred literature of the world there is preserved the teaching of a Way or Path, known to the seekers of all ages.

The present book is concerned with outlining this Way which, according to the records, is a process of transforming man's entire being, and this process is traced, stage by stage, through its expression in symbols and images, common to all great religious traditions. The spiral, the wilderness, the labyrinth, the wheel, the rose, the tree, fire and light are such images which are all produced, and reacted to, spontaneously by those who travel on this Way of self-transcendence.

'A wealth of wisdom and knowledge are apparent in this most perceptive approach to comparative religion from the life side.' *Theosophical Journal*.

THE LORE OF THE UNICORN

ODELL SHEPARD

'Odell Shepard', declared one reviewer when this book was first published, 'is a scholarly hunter of the wildest and most elusive game'. His quarry, and his delight, has been the Unicorn, and he has pursued the trail of this strange beast through mythology, folklore, magic, medicine, literature, art, exploration, poisoning and the history of commerce. Urbane and lucid in its presentation, the book is also a storehouse of arcane and curious lore. But the 'holy hunt' is not treated as an end in itself: the Unicorn becomes for Mr Shepard a single, vivid example of 'the ways by which magic rose into religious dogma and this gradually succumbed, or is succumbing, under the attrition of modern science'.

'A fascinating and exciting record . . . Mr Odell Shepard is a scholarly hunter of the wildest and most elusive game.' *Times*

'Scholarly, extraordinarily readable and has very many peculiarly good illustrations.' *New Statesman*

'What a book! . . . His text is so delightful, so widely ranging in its allusions, so full of odd facts and discreetly humorous comment . . . that it can be read forward from any point, or even backwards, by any person who has in him any grain of the poet or of the curious scholar . . .' *The Observer*

'Enchanting . . . Extraordinarily picturesque . . . A book to dip into again and again.' *Sunday Times*

MYTH AND REALITY
MIRCEA ELIADE

There are two ways to interpret the word 'myth' today. Either it is taken to mean a 'fable', 'invention' or 'fiction', or, as Eliade uses it, to mean a true story that is most precious because it is sacred, exemplary and significant. Eliade's new book deals primarily with those societies in which myth is—or was until very recently—a living force, in the sense of supplying models for human behaviour and, by that very fact, giving meaning and value to daily life. To understand the structure and function of myth in these traditional societies serves not only to clarify a stage in the history of human thought, but also helps us to understand certain contemporary societies. Even further, it illuminates that subconscious region of the mind where the all-encompassing certainty of myth is still an active element.

Dr Eliade takes his examples from all cultures and all continents. He describes the myths of creation, of death and renewal, of the end of the world, the mystery of time, etc., as they are experienced by Polynesians, Australian aborigines, Greeks, Romans, Egyptians and many others. And in the last chapters he describes the grandeur and decadence of myths and how they survive under camouflage in our own day in the various forms of political ideologies, psycho-analysis and avant-garde art.

MANY VOICES
EILEEN J. GARRETT

Eileen J. Garrett is a unique woman, and *Many Voices* is an unforgettable testament and testimony – an adventure into the paranormal world – for this is the autobiography of the greatest practising medium in the world today. This is a vivid and fascinating story, and one which has remained untold for too long. Internationally renowned for her extraordinary powers of clairvoyance and telepathy, widely recognized by the scientific community for her experiments with psychic phenomena, Eileen J. Garrett tells the complete story of her public and private life.

'. . . the contents of this book are so stimulating and thought-provoking that the opportunity of reading it should on no account be missed.'
Psychical Studies

LONDON: GEORGE ALLEN AND UNWIN LTD